DK Pocket Genius

BIRDS OF
NORTH AMERICA

FACTS AT YOUR FINGERTIPS

Senior Art Editor Shreya Anand
Project Editor Kathakali Banerjee
Project Editor Mansi Agrawal
Editorial team Arpit Aggarwal, Deeksha Micek
Art Editors Sifat Fatima, Aparajita Sen
US Editor Jill Hamilton
Assistant Picture Researcher Mayank Choudhary
Managing Editor Kingshuk Ghoshal
Managing Art Editor Govind Mittal
DTP Designers Vijay Kandwal, Rakesh Kumar
Production Editor Shanker Prasad
Senior Production Controller Jude Crozier
Jacket Designer Vidushi Chaudhry
Jacket Design Development Manager Sophia MTT
Publisher Andrew Macintyre
Associate Publishing Director Liz Wheeler
Art Director Karen Self
Publishing Director Jonathan Metcalf

Author Derek Harvey
Consultant Stephen W. Kress

First American Edition, 2022
Published in the United States by DK Publishing
1745 Broadway, 20th Floor, New York, NY 10019

Copyright © 2022 Dorling Kindersley Limited
DK, a Division of Penguin Random House LLC
22 23 24 25 26 10 9 8 7 6 5 4 3 2 1
001–328714–Aug/2022

A catalog record for this book
is available from the Library of Congress.
ISBN: 978-0-7440-5808-6

DK books are available at special discounts when
purchased in bulk for sales promotions, premiums,
fund-raising, or educational use. For details, contact:
DK Publishing Special Markets,
1745 Broadway, 20th Floor, New York, NY 10019
SpecialSales@dk.com

Printed and bound in Latvia

For the curious

www.dk.com

Scales and sizes
This book contains profiles of
birds with scale drawings to show
their size.

 6 ft
(1.8 m)

 6.3 in
(16 cm)

Map
Each bird profile includes a map
showing the range of the species
in the US and Canada. The colors
denote seasonal movements.

Lives all year round

Summer range

Winter range

Seen on migration

Habitats
The main habitats for each bird
profile are shown as symbols. Find
out more about them on pp.14–15.

 Mountains   Wetlands

Broadleaf
and mixed
forests

Mangrove
swamps

 Coniferous
forests

Coastal
areas

 Open
habitats

Seas and
oceans

Deserts

Tundra and
polar regions

 Freshwater
bodies

 Human
habitats

Endangered birds
This label indicates that the bird is
in danger of dying out, as per IUCN.
Find out about the
Red List on p.16.   **ENDANGERED**

CONTENTS

Sex symbols

♀ Female   ♂ Male

No symbol used if the male and female of a species look alike

What is a bird?

Feathers make birds unmistakable: no other kind of living thing has them. But these vertebrates (animals with a backbone) do share some features with other animals. They are warm-blooded, like mammals, but lay eggs, like most reptiles. And the fact that they walk upright on two scaly, clawed feet is a reminder of their dinosaur ancestors.

Bony skeleton

Many features of a bird's skeleton are related to the fact that most can fly. Their hollow bones are lightweight, their arm bones are used as wings, and a large breast bone carries muscles for flapping the wings.

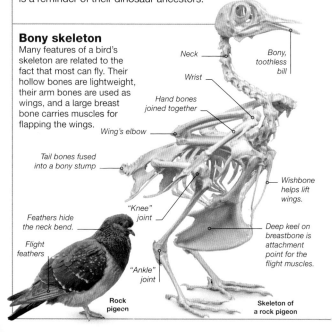

Neck

Bony, toothless bill

Wrist

Hand bones joined together

Wing's elbow

Tail bones fused into a bony stump

Feathers hide the neck bend.

Flight feathers

"Knee" joint

"Ankle" joint

Wishbone helps lift wings.

Deep keel on breastbone is attachment point for the flight muscles.

Rock pigeon

Skeleton of a rock pigeon

Living dinosaurs

Birds evolved from two-legged predatory dinosaurs called theropods, a group that included the non-flying *Velociraptor*. Some of these theropods had feathers. *Archaeopteryx* was an early bird. Over time, birds acquired a toothless bill and lost the claws on their "hands."

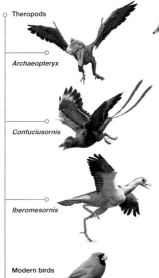

Theropods

Archaeopteryx

Confuciusornis

Iberomesornis

Modern birds

Bird features

The feathers of birds evolved from the scales of their reptile ancestors. Their eggs have hard, brittle shells—in contrast to the leathery-shelled eggs laid by most reptiles.

Flight feathers

Down feathers trap heat.

Feathers help trap body warmth, shed water, give birds their color, and form their stiff flight feathers.

Warm-blooded birds must sit on their eggs, usually in a nest, to incubate them (keep the eggs warm until they hatch).

Types of birds

There are more than 10,000 species of birds in the world today and about 3,000 of them are found in North America. Scientists classify birds that are related into groups called orders. Each order is then split into smaller groups, called families, that contain species that are more closely related.

Bird orders

The basic groups, or orders, separate birds with the most distinct body shapes and lifestyles—such as waterfowl with their ducklike bills and owls with their big, forward-facing eyes. Most chapters in this book cover birds from several orders. But one order—the passerine birds—has a chapter of its own.

Fowl, pigeons, and relatives
This chapter covers four orders—land fowl, waterfowl, grebes, and pigeons.

Cuckoos, nightjars, swifts, and hummingbirds
One order contains the cuckoos, a second contains the nightjars, and a third has the swifts and hummingbirds.

Rails, shorebirds, and relatives
One order contains cranes, rails, and relatives, and a second one contains shorebirds, gulls, and auks.

Seabirds, herons, and relatives
This chapter spans five orders of waterbirds, represented by albatrosses, cormorants, herons, storks, and loons.

Bird families

Most orders contain eight families or less, but the passerines—the biggest order—has more than 130, and contains more than two-thirds of all bird species. Birds from different families often eat different things—such as seed-eaters in the sparrow family and insect-eaters in the tyrant family.

Broad, insect-catching bill

Long tail streamers

Scissor-tailed flycatcher from the tyrant family

Bird names

Indigo bunting
Passerina cyanea

Painted bunting
Passerina ciris

In addition to its common English name, each species has a two-word Latin name, such as *Passerina ciris* for the painted bunting. The Latin name means the same to scientists that speak different languages. Species that are very closely related share the same first part of this name, so the indigo bunting is called *Passerina cyanea*.

Barn owl

Vultures, hawks, eagles, and owls
American vultures belong to one order, hawks and eagles to a second, and owls to a third.

Pileated woodpecker

Kingfishers, woodpeckers, and falcons
This chapter covers three orders, represented by kingfishers, woodpeckers, and falcons.

Yellow warbler

Passerines
The single order of passerines includes many familiar perching birds, such as crows, tits, warblers, and sparrows.

Body and flight

Almost everything about a bird is geared toward an energetic lifestyle that involves flying. Birds have a fast, strong heart, a short, stiff body packed with big chest muscles for powering flapping wings, and good senses for finding food and spotting danger.

Body parts

Except for the feet and beak, all parts of a bird's body are usually covered in feathers. On most of the body are small, soft contour feathers, while longer, stiffer flight feathers make up the wings and tail.

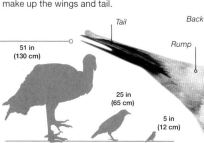

Wing flight feathers

Tail

Back

Rump

51 in
(130 cm)

25 in
(65 cm)

5 in
(12 cm)

California
condor

Common
raven

American
goldfinch

Thigh

*Tarsus
(leg)*

Belly

Size

Most birds are small, which makes it easier for them to take off and stay in the air, but there are also some giants. At 22 lb (10 kg)—the weight of a mountain bike—the California condor is one of the biggest birds in North America.

Staying airborne

It takes a lot of flapping wing power for a big bird to take to the skies, but once there, birds such as the turkey vulture save energy by soaring on winds.

Broad wings catch the wind.

Covert feathers

Crown

Forehead

Bill

Chin

Throat

Breast

American goldfinch about to land

Migration

Flight means that birds can travel long-distance migrations. During cold northern winters, when insects or other food decline, many birds such as the common yellowthroat fly south to the tropics, where their food is abundant all year round.

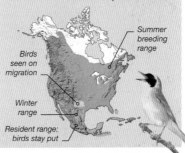

Summer breeding range

Birds seen on migration

Winter range

Resident range: birds stay put

Birdwatching

Some birds are easier to identify than others, but there are lots of clues that you can use to tell one kind from another—their size and shape, color and markings (called "field marks"), sounds and movements, habitat, and time of year are all important.

Color and pattern

A bird's colors can be very showy or blend in so well with the background that they are well hidden. Colors can change a lot as a bird grows to breeding maturity, and the sexes can look very different too. Breeding males usually have the brightest colors, while young and females are less colorful.

Female wood duck has brown-gray plumage and a large white eye-ring.

Colors can appear dark or faint depending on the light, but patterns and markings are often unmistakable. For instance, the Wilson's storm-petrel is a small bird of the open seas, but the white patches on its dark body can be distinctive—even from a distance.

♂ **Breeding male wood duck has bold colored markings and a large U-shape patch on its neck.**

♀

Sound and movement

Birds that lack bright colors may be detected in other ways. Many birds are more likely to be heard than seen—such as the booming bittern or singing wood thrush. Some have a special behavior—such as the brown creeper that climbs up, then flies down to the base of another tree.

A wood thrush sings its flutelike song at dawn and dusk.

A brown creeper can climb up a trunk or come down backward.

Bills

A bird uses its bill to collect food, so the shape and size of a bill not only helps identify a bird, but may also say something about the kinds of things that it eats.

Pileated woodpecker

A strong, pointed chisel-like bill is used to hammer tree bark for insects or excavate a nest.

Broad-billed hummingbird

A long thin bill is used to probe flowers so the hummingbird can drink nectar.

Northern cardinal

A strong, chunky bill, is used to crack open fruit and seeds.

Osprey

A sharply hooked bill is used to tear flesh—in this case, to eat fish.

Feet

All birds have scaly feet with clawed toes. But many use their feet for running or digging, others for swimming or perching— and some even as weapons.

Canada goose

Webbed feet are used for pushing back in water—to propel the bird forward when swimming.

American coot

Separately webbed toes are used for swimming, but are also good for walking on wet ground.

Common raven

Clawed toes—three in front and one behind—are good for gripping a branch when perching.

Bald eagle

Sharply curved talons are used to grab prey with a killing grip.

Raising a family

It takes care and know-how to bring up a baby—and birds can be especially good at it. But family life in birds varies a lot. Some chicks are looked after by mom and dad, while in others just one parent takes charge. And some chicks hatch blind and helpless in a protective nest, while others can run and feed for themselves almost immediately.

Mates and courtship

Adult birds show off to others—with song, color, or even dance—to attract a mate, and sometimes seal a partnership that might help them raise a family together.

Males have a thicker bill than females.

Stiffly bent neck

Wings held upright

♂

♀

The "rushing ceremony" of the western grebe involves two courting birds splashing across water—before the male mates with the female.

Nests and eggs

A few birds lay their eggs on bare ground, but most build some kind of nest—such as a hole in a tree or this soft cup made by a female eastern phoebe, a small, insect-eating woodland bird. She has woven it from fine grass, moss, mud, and leaves.

Clutches and chicks

Some birds lay a single egg, but others lay many more, so end up with bigger families. More eggs mean more chicks might survive, but parents might have to work harder to look after them. Chicks that hatch naked and helpless are described as altricial. Feathered ones that can walk soon after hatching are precocial.

An American robin's altricial chicks are blind and naked when they hatch, but they grow quickly on worms, opening their eyes and sprouting feathers.

Chicks beg for food with gaping mouths.

Becoming adult

Chick feathers are fluffier than adult ones. As they grow into older youngsters, called juveniles, they develop stiffer flight feathers to fly—a process called fledging. Juvenile birds often have duller colors than adult ones.

Downy feathers help keep the chick warm.

Adults have smoother outer feathers, some of which help with flight.

Laughing gull chick

Laughing gull adult

Where birds live

North American birds have found ways to survive on the bleakest Arctic land and the highest mountains. They fly the skies along the coastlines and fill the forests and prairies. Some birds have even adapted to the newest habitats—the farmland, towns, and cities created by humans.

Range

The range covered by this book includes mainland Canada and the US—as well as the seas that can be seen around their coastlines.

Habitats

A few birds are very adaptable and can survive in places as different as forests and deserts. But most rely on particular kinds of habitats to find food and breed.

Mountains
Trees cannot grow on the highest mountaintops, so the birds survive on an open, rocky landscape.

Broadleaf and mixed forests
Most broadleaf trees, such as oaks, lose their leaves in winter, but may be mixed with evergreen conifers.

Freshwater bodies
Ponds, lakes, rivers, and streams are freshwater habitats that are home to waterbirds.

Wetlands
Grasslands and woodlands that are flooded—permanently or seasonally—are called wetlands.

Mangrove swamps
Some trees—called mangroves—can grow on muddy coastlines, where they get flooded by the tide.

🏙️ Human habitats

For many birds, our buildings are just like cliffs, caves, and rock faces—a perfect spot for making a high-rise nest that is well away from predators and other danger.

A peregrine falcon raises its chicks on a skyscraper ledge.

Introduced birds

Some kinds of birds that live in the wild in North America originally came from other parts of the world. Starlings and house sparrows were deliberately introduced from Britain and are now commonly found across the continent.

European starling

Coniferous forests
Most conifers have evergreen, needlelike leaves and dominate some kinds of forest, such as in the cold north.

Open habitats
Habitats with few trees include grasslands and fields, as well as places with low scrubby bushes.

Deserts
Some habitats are too dry for grassland and forest, but have desert plants such as cacti and desert scrubs.

Coastal areas
Shorelines, beaches, cliffs, and the seas visible from shore are included in coastal areas.

Seas and oceans
A few kinds of birds live so far out at sea that they are true "ocean" species.

Tundra and polar regions
Arctic seas have floating ice, while nearby land, with frozen ground, has open habitat called tundra.

Birds under threat

Birds need the right sort of habitat, free from danger, to live and breed. But lots of things can reduce their numbers—and some species have been affected so much that they could disappear altogether (become extinct). Pollution, hunting, and even our own pets can all take a heavy toll.

Threatened species

Every kind of bird is in an online Red List (see p.150), where scientists have graded their levels of threat—from the least concern to the most critically endangered.

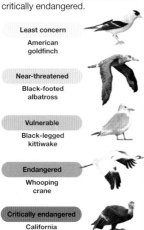

Least concern

American goldfinch

Near-threatened

Black-footed albatross

Vulnerable

Black-legged kittiwake

Endangered

Whooping crane

Critically endangered

California condor

Extinct birds

Some birds—including the labrador duck—that once lived in North America have been completely wiped out by hunting or habitat loss.

Labrador duck

Pollution

As burning fossil fuels poisons the air and causes global warming, habitats such as mountainous coniferous forests die back—reducing the home range of Bicknell's thrush and other species found nowhere else.

Bicknell's thrush

Disappearing habitats and hunting

Natural habitats are cleared to make way for cities, towns, and farms, while some birds have been hunted for their feathers or meat. Both threats have driven birds, such as the whooping crane, almost to extinction.

Cranes fly with their legs trailing behind them.

Black wing tips

Fitted with a radio transmitter to track movement

Outstretched neck

The whooping crane flies long distances in its migration, which makes it vulnerable as it crosses more land.

Hazards near home

Many birds adapt to our towns and cities, and some even nest on our buildings. But each year, billions of birds are killed by our pet cats—or by flying into windows.

A pet cat watches mourning doves eat birdseed from a window ledge.

Helping birds

We can do a great deal to help birds—even at our own doorstep. Bird feeders, nest boxes, and wildlife-friendly gardens mean more birds survive and breed from year to year. In the long run, this helps entire species. When setting up bird feeders and nest boxes, it helps to keep cats indoors.

Slanted roof drains rain away from nest hole.

Ruby-throated hummingbird at a sugar feeder

♂

Male eastern bluebird visits a nest built by a female.

American goldfinches at a tube feeder in summer

Feeding birds

Bird feeders provide extra nourishment for birds and so can help them survive when natural supplies run short. This is especially important in winter, when birds need more fuel to keep warm.

Nest boxes

Artificial nest boxes help when natural nesting sites are in short supply. Some— with small entrance holes— are for birds that use tree cavities. Others are more open for birds that nest on branches.

Female eastern bluebird

♀

Put up stickers on windows that will help birds avoid collisions with the windows.

Improving habitats

Backyards, gardens, and parks often have plants that do not supply good food or nesting sites for North American birds. But by planting native trees and shrubs that produce nuts and seeds, we can make our gardens more bird-friendly.

Blue jays eat acorns from native oak trees in winter.

Bird reserves

Governments and other conservation groups set aside areas of the country to protect habitats, such as wetlands and forests, that many birds rely on to feed, breed, or spend the winter.

American white pelicans stop over on the Riverlands Sanctuary in Missouri during their migration.

Fowl, pigeons, and relatives

Land fowl, such as turkeys, and waterfowl, such as ducks, are groups that include many birds that spend lots of time on land or water. Land fowl don't fly far, but many waterfowl fly long distances in their migration. Grebes and pigeons are more distantly related—grebes are waterbirds, while pigeons live in a variety of land habitats.

SIZABLE SWAN
Swans are giants among waterfowl. The trumpeter swan—North America's biggest waterfowl species—can weigh up to 35 lb (15.8 kg).

FOCUS ON...
FORAGING

Swans, geese and surface ducks eat plants, but most diving ducks, such as mergansers, hunt for fish and other aquatic prey—disappearing right underwater to catch a meal.

▲ An extra-long neck helps swans probe for water plants.

▲ "Dabbling" ducks, such as mallards, upend to nibble on aquatic plants.

Waterfowl

With webbed feet, a broad flat "duckbill," and, in geese and swans, a long neck, waterfowl are easy to recognize. Most of them are expert swimmers.

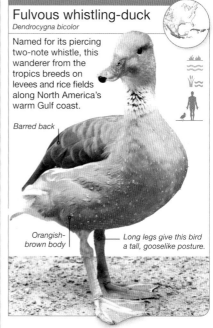

Fulvous whistling-duck
Dendrocygna bicolor

Named for its piercing two-note whistle, this wanderer from the tropics breeds on levees and rice fields along North America's warm Gulf coast.

Barred back

Orangish-brown body

Long legs give this bird a tall, gooselike posture.

Tundra swan
Cygnus columbianus

After nesting in the summer Arctic, this swan migrates south to spend the winter on fields and marshlands, especially near the coast.

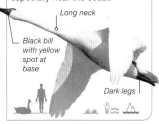

Long neck

Black bill with yellow spot at base

Dark legs

Snow goose
Anser caerulescens

This Arctic breeder has two color forms—one is all white and the other is gray-brown with a white head.

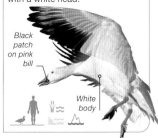

Black patch on pink bill

White body

Canada goose
Branta canadensis

Like other species of geese, the Canada goose gets most of its food by grazing on grassland, but usually near water.

Prominent white chin patch

Wood duck
Aix sponsa

This woodland duck nests in holes in trees, so flightless chicks must take a long tumble to the ground after hatching. Males have a distinct green and purple face, but females have a gray head with a white eye-ring.

♂

Northern shoveler
Spatula clypeata

With its wide bill, this bird scoops large mouthfuls of food, including pondweed, snails, and insect larvae. Females are a mottled brown color.

♂

Mallard
Anas platyrhynchos

Metallic green head in males, gray-brown in females

White ring around neck

♂

Like other related ducks, the mallard has a bold metallic patch of color (speculum) on its wings. This may work like a signal to keep a flock together, especially when flying.

Violet-blue wing patch

American wigeon

Mareca americana

The American wigeon is a medium-sized dabbling duck. It has a shorter bill than most ducks, and a squeaking high-pitched *whew-whew-whew* call, rather than a quacking voice.

White underwing

Pinkish-brown flanks

White forehead

Green band at the back of the eye in males, gray-brown head in females

♂

Wandering American wigeons may reach Britain by flying over the Atlantic Ocean.

White belly contrasts with rest of brown body.

Common merganser
Mergus merganser

The common merganser's bill, which has sawlike edges and a sharply hooked tip, helps this diving bird grip slippery fish that it catches underwater—after dipping its head at the surface and scanning the depths for a target.

Brown head in females, greenish-black in males

Both sexes have a red bill that gets duller in winter.

Dark outer wing

♀

Surf scoter
Melanitta perspicillata

After breeding in cold northern lakes surrounded by pine trees, this duck flies toward the sea, where it winters along coasts and in estuaries.

Large triangular bill is orange and white in males, dark gray in females

Both sexes have white patches on top and back of head.

♂

Long-tailed duck
Clangula hyemalis

White head with dark neck patch

♂

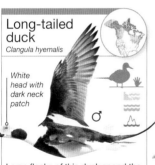

Large flocks of this duck spend the winter diving for shellfish. In this season, males are mainly white, females grayer; both have a blacker head in summer.

King eider
Somateria spectabilis

One of the most northerly of American birds, the king eider nests in the summer Arctic tundra, and spends the rest of the year at sea.

Colorful head and bill in breeding males

♂

Land fowl

Quails, turkeys, grouse, and relatives are weaker fliers than waterfowl and spend much of their time on land. Many have mottled brown plumage to help camouflage them, but when it's time to breed males strut to impress the females.

Northern bobwhite
Colinus virginianus

Except when paired off and breeding, this land fowl gathers in groups, or coveys, that can number over 20 birds. It gets its name from its whistling *bob-white* call.

White throat in males, light brown in females

♂

Black barring on underparts

California quail
Callipepla californica

The state bird of California shows off its flaglike crest in courtship displays. Browner females have a shorter crest and gray face.

Crest has six comma-shaped feathers.

♂

Wild turkey
Meleagris gallopavo

The ancestor of domesticated turkeys is more lightweight and agile. Males usually grow larger than females.

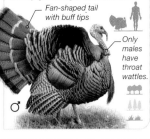

Fan-shaped tail with buff tips

Only males have throat wattles.

♂

Ruffed grouse
Bonasa umbellus

Grouse tend to eat more plants than other land fowl. During the winter, the ruffed grouse survives almost entirely on the flower buds of aspen trees.

Males raise neck feathers like a ruff in a display.

♂

Rock ptarmigan
Lagopus muta

In winter, the rock ptarmigan changes its brown-speckled plumage for an all-white one that provides better camouflage when it snows.

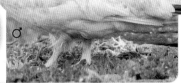

Fleshy red comb above the eye is larger in males.

Dark feathers are replaced by white winter feathers during a molt.

Rock ptarmigans can be seen at heights of up to 6,560 ft (2,000 m) on Canadian mountains.

♂

Grebes

Well adapted for life on water—with paddling feet set far back on their body—grebes cannot easily walk on land. Their unconnected toes have flat lobes to push through water.

Pied-billed grebe
Podilymbus podiceps

Like other species of grebes, the pied-billed grebe hunts for small animals by diving underwater. It dips under for a few seconds to grab insects, shrimp, and frogs—and sometimes even leeches.

Whitish bill with distinctive black stripe

Reddish-brown neck

Red-necked grebe
Podiceps grisegena

In summer, the red-necked grebe breeds on pools by building floating nests made from vegetation. It spends winter on the coasts or on the open sea.

Gray-white "ear" feathers stand out when breeding.

Horned grebe
Podiceps auritus

Dark "ear" feathers contrast with yellow head tufts.

The yellow feathery head tufts of this species stick up like horns during the breeding season. Like most other species of grebes, its winter plumage is less colorful—it turns black and white, although its eyes stay bright red.

Reddish-brown neck

Western grebe
Aechmophorus occidentalis

The western grebe has a spectacular "rushing" display in which courting pairs or two rival males stretch upright and run, side by side, noisily over the surface of a lake. The black on the head of this bird extends in front of its eyes.

Prominent red eyes

White underparts contrast sharply with dark head and back.

Pigeons and doves

Birds in the pigeon-dove family, many of which are at home in our towns, are easily recognized by the way their small heads bob up and down when they walk or while they are perched.

Common ground dove
Columbina passerina

The smallest dove in North America—and one of the smallest worldwide—spends much of its time pecking for seeds and other food on the ground. It often wanders over town lawns and can make an appearance at bird feeders and water holes in the southern US.

Dark edges to feathers give the underparts a scaly appearance in both sexes.

Male doves have a pinkish-brown breast.

♀

Black patches on wings

♂

Mourning dove
Zenaida macroura

One of the commonest birds on the continent, this dove thrives on agricultural land. It is a fast breeder and can nest and raise a family within a year of hatching.

Black dot on side of the face

Female has paler head and neck than male

Plain, light brown underparts in both sexes

♂

Band-tailed pigeon
Patagioenas fasciata

The band-tailed pigeon relies on oak and pine woodland, where it can get plenty of its favorite food—acorns. When the acorns run out in winter, it turns to berries and grain. This bird is North America's largest pigeon—it can grow up to 16 in (40 cm) long.

Metallic greenish-bronze patch bordered by white stripe

Yellow feet

Dark band across tail

Cuckoos, nightjars, swifts, and hummingbirds

Strong-billed cuckoos, such as the ground-living roadrunner, can tackle large prey, but other birds in these groups have more delicate tastes— nightjars and swifts catch flying insects, while hummingbirds drink nectar.

TINY BIRD
Hummingbirds are among the world's smallest birds. Anna's hummingbird builds a nest that is smaller than an egg cup.

Cuckoos

North American cuckoos either build their own nests, or use the nests of other kinds of birds—such as thrushes, blackbirds, or other species of cuckoos.

Greater roadrunner

Geococcyx californianus

Although it flies well, this long-tailed member of the cuckoo family prefers to sprint over the ground after prey, including tarantulas, scorpions, and rattlesnakes.

Long tail with white edges may be cocked up and then slowly lowered.

Large crest

Shaggy plumage

Large bill helps the roadrunner grip big prey.

Streaked back and wings

Long legs help the bird outrun prey, even the fastest lizards.

Black-billed cuckoo
Coccyzus erythropthalmus

In summer, the black-billed cuckoos have a distinctive *cucucu-cucucu-cucucu* cry—an example of a call that gives a bird its name.

Red eye-ring

White underparts

White spots on tips of tail feathers

Yellow-billed cuckoo
Coccyzus americanus

Both the yellow-billed and black-billed cuckoos build a nest out of sticks. But sometimes these two species will lay their eggs—which are greenish-blue in both cases—in each other's nests. They end up raising chicks that don't belong to them.

Eye-ring is yellow or grayish.

Reddish-brown outer wing

Nightjars and swifts

These birds are experts at catching flying insects on the wing—and can open their mouths wide to collect them. Nighthawks and nightjars fly at night, while day-flying swifts are so comfortable in the skies that they even sleep there.

FOCUS ON...
PREYING

Special adaptations help nighthawks and nightjars catch insects on moonlit nights or at dusk and dawn.

▲ A light-reflecting layer, which makes their eyes shine, improves vision in low light.

▲ Bristles around the bill may help guide insects into their wide mouth.

Common nighthawk
Chordeiles minor

The common nighthawk is expert at catching insects high in the night sky and might gather in flocks of hundreds when there are plenty of insects to catch. It also preys on moths drawn to artificial lights.

White throat in males, absent in females

♂

White wing patch

Courting males do dive-bomb displays and make booming sounds with their wings in flight.

Common poorwill
Phalaenoptilus nuttallii

Like other insect-eating birds, North American nighthawks and their relatives migrate south in winter, except for the poorwill, which is the only bird known to hibernate. Its plumage camouflages and protects it as it sleeps among rocks.

Brown-speckled body plumage

Short, white-edged tail

Chimney swift
Chaetura pelagica

In the past, this species probably bred in tree holes. Today, it prefers to do so in dark chimneys, where it glues sticks into a nest using its own spit.

Short, spiny tail

White-throated swift
Aeronautes saxatalis

The white-throated swift hunts and breeds along rocky cliffs, where it flies in noisy shrilling colonies.

White throat contrasts with dark uppparts.

Hummingbirds can fly more than

2,500 miles

(4,000 km) on their migration across North America

HURTLING HUMMINGBIRDS
The calliope hummingbird (left) and rufous hummingbird (right) migrate from their overwintering grounds in Mexico as far north as Canada, and time their arrival for when nectar-providing flowers are blooming.

Hummingbirds

The smallest birds need a lot of fuel to keep their tiny bodies working—and hummingbirds get it by lapping sweet nectar from flowers with their long tongue. Expert at hovering, they can appear to be motionless in the air while they probe each bloom.

Ruby-throated hummingbird

Archilochus colubris

North America's most widespread hummingbird overwinters in warmer Central America, where it relies on plenty of fat-rich insect food to accompany sips of nectar.

Ruby-red throat in males

Tiny feet for perching

♂

Rufous hummingbird

Selasphorus rufus

The rufous hummingbird migrates over the Rocky Mountains and deserts between its summer breeding range and winter range, stopping to refuel at flowers along the way.

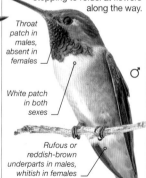

Throat patch in males, absent in females

White patch in both sexes

Rufous or reddish-brown underparts in males, whitish in females

♂

FOCUS ON...
HOVERING

A hummingbird's wings sweep back and forth in one smooth path.

▲ Wings swinging backward helps lift the bird up against gravity.

▲ Wingtips twist in readiness to swing forward.

▲ Wings swing forward, maintaining the lift to keep the bird in the air.

Anna's hummingbird
Calypte anna

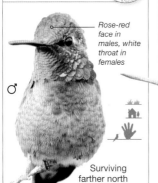

Rose-red face in males, white throat in females

♂

Surviving farther north than many other hummingbirds, this species has expanded its range in recent decades. It has adapted to the cold in the north and regularly takes advantage of garden feeders in winter.

Costa's hummingbird
Calypte costae

A bird of dry open deserts, Costa's hummingbird sometimes nests in spiny cacti. Like other species, it fiercely defends flowers in its territory from other nectar-feeders.

Violet throat feathers in males

Long bill

♂

Rails, shorebirds, and relatives

Rails and shorebirds, such as stilts, have long legs for wading in mud or shallow water for food. Their unwebbed toes are perfect for walking or gripping vegetation. But others, such as coastal gulls and auks, rely more on fishing out at sea, using their webbed feet to swim easily in water.

CARRYING A MOUTHFUL
The bill of a puffin develops colors to impress a mate and it can carry lots of fish at once back to hungry chicks.

Rails and relatives

Most species of rails are secretive birds that spend a lot of time hiding in marshes and other wetland habitats. Their brown and gray colors make them difficult to spot. But their relatives, such as gallinules and coots, are bolder and swim in open water.

Purple gallinule
Porphyrio martinicus

The purple gallinule walks on floating vegetation, occasionally flipping over waterlily leaves to look for animal prey, such as snails, which supplement its diet of mainly aquatic plants. The bird's colors make it stand out.

Pale blue shield above red bill

This bird might sometimes gobble up chicks of other waterbirds, such as herons.

Sora
Porzana carolina

More often heard than seen, this wetland bird makes a squeaking call to defend its territory during the breeding season.

Black mask with yellow bill

Purple plumage turns bluer on the back.

Dark blue belly

Large yellow feet help the gallinule climb vegetation.

Virginia rail
Rallus limicola

The long bill of this rail is perfect for probing mud and vegetation for prey, including worms, snails, insects, and sometimes frogs or small snakes.

Gray face contrasts with body

Streaks on upperparts

American coot
Fulica americana

With paddlelike feet, coots swim on the water like ducks, then dive beneath the surface in search of food, such as pondweed, insects, and snails.

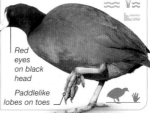

Red eyes on black head

Paddlelike lobes on toes

Limpkin and cranes

Cranes are large birds of open places, such as grasslands and wetlands. They have loud haunting calls and elegant courtship dances. A smaller cousin is the limpkin, which is more at home in warm swamps along the Gulf coast.

FOCUS ON... COURTSHIP

Crane courtship dances involve a lot of jumping and wing-stretching as partners try to impress one another.

▲ A "bill-up" display of a pair of sandhill cranes helps attract attention.

▲ Leaping upward seals the partnership before mating.

Limpkin
Aramus guarauna

The limpkin feeds almost entirely on pond snails and mussels. Its long bill has a sharp tip that helps remove their flesh easily from the shells.

Dark brown wings with white spots

Long legs enable the bird to wade easily in water.

Sandhill crane
Antigone canadensis

The sandhill crane is the most abundant of the world's crane species. Hundreds of thousands of sandhill cranes live in North America. Birds nesting in the north migrate long distances when flying south in the winter.

Bare skin on the forehead looks like a bright red crown.

Whooping crane

ENDANGERED

Grus americana

Standing 5 ft (1.5 m) high, the whooping crane is North America's tallest bird. It has a distinct red crown and a black marking on its face that looks like a moustache. It is endangered, but conservation efforts have helped increase its numbers.

The whooping crane gets its name from its buglelike call, whooping call.

Snowy white body

Long, gray-black legs

Stilts, oystercatchers, and plovers

These shorebirds have bills shaped for feeding in different ways. Stilts have long, thin bills for probing, while plovers have shorter ones for jabbing the ground.

American avocet
Recurvirostra americana

By sweeping its long, upturned-curved bill—like a scythe—through water or along the surface of mud, an American avocet can grab lots of tiny animal prey in a few seconds.

Bill has tiny ridges that help trap food.

Orange-brown head and neck

White belly turns pinkish when breeding.

Day-old avocets can walk, swim, and even dive to escape predators.

Black-necked stilt
Himantopus mexicanus

Extra-long legs help this stilt wade into deep wetland water, where it plucks tiny swimming animals, such as insects and shrimp.

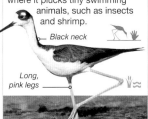

Black neck

Long, pink legs

American oystercatcher
Haematopus palliatus

Yellow eyes

Red bill helps open shells easily.

The American oystercatcher plunges its bill into a mussel and then snips to remove the fleshy animal before it has a chance to close its shell.

Killdeer
Charadrius vociferus

The killdeer is more at home inland than other plovers—wandering onto fields or even golf courses in search of food. It stamps the ground to flush out small prey, such as insects, spiders, and worms.

White neck collar

Two black bands across the breast

Sandpipers and relatives

Many of these birds breed on cold Arctic tundra in summer but then fly south to overwinter on coastlines and wetlands, where they gather in large flocks. Their earth-colored winter plumage can be a good camouflage on mudflats and sand.

FOCUS ON... FEEDING

Long, pointed bills are perfect for catching small animal prey, such as worms, shrimp, and tiny fishes.

▲ The greater yellowlegs sweeps its bill through water to fish.

▲ The long-billed curlew probes deeply in soft mud for food.

Long-billed curlew
Numenius americanus

During the breeding season, this bird nests in clumps of grass on prairies and meadows, where it preys on insects. It then switches to burrowing prey, such as shrimp and crabs, while it spends the winter on muddy coasts and estuaries.

Males take care of the young as the females leave their chicks within 2–3 weeks of hatching.

Feathers are cinnamon colored.

Short tail

♀

Females have a longer bill with a more distinct curve at the tip than males.

Marbled godwit
Limosa fedoa

Like many of its relatives, the marbled godwit develops more intense colors when breeding inland—then turns duller in winter.

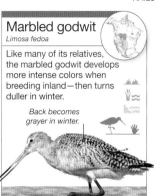

Back becomes grayer in winter.

Ruddy turnstone
Arenaria interpres

As its name suggests, this bird flips over stones, shells, and seaweed to look for prey beneath.

Reddish-brown back when breeding

Least sandpiper
Calidris minutilla

Needlelike bill

The world's smallest shorebird has an impressive migration. After breeding on Arctic tundra, it flies to South America, where it spends winter in the vast Amazon wetlands.

Short, straw-coloured legs

As many as

half a million

dunlins overwinter on the Pacific coast of North America

AMERICAN WADERS
Winter flocks of dunlins can contain tens of thousands of birds that are attracted to coastal mudflats, where they refuel on buried worms after the long migration from their Arctic tundra breeding grounds.

Long-billed dowitcher
Limnodromus scolopaceus

The long-billed dowitcher is an Arctic breeder that spends winter mostly in freshwater habitats, such as marshes around the edges of lakes.

Long, stout bill helps probe deep in mud.

Reddish-brown belly when breeding

Wilson's snipe
Gallinago delicata

Like other kinds of snipes, this bird prefers to stick to the cover of grasses when feeding, rather than in the open like sandpipers. It is most often spotted when it flies up and calls when it is disturbed.

Long, pointed wings

Dark brown barring on plumage

Bill probes soggy ground for prey.

Short tail

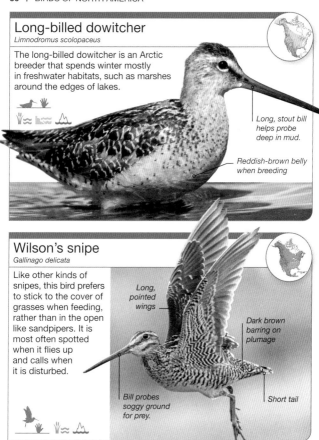

Greater yellowlegs
Tringa melanoleuca

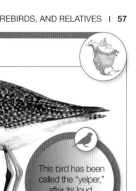

Long legs help
this species
wade
deeper than many
other shorebirds,
where it uses its long bill
to catch small animals
swimming in open water.

*White belly develops black
spots when breeding.*

Long, yellow legs

This bird has been
called the "yelper,"
after its loud,
piercing call.

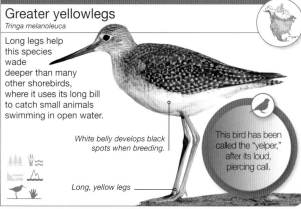

Red-necked phalarope
Phalaropus lobatus

Unusual for birds, phalarope
females have brighter colors
than males. Females fight over
territory, leaving males to
incubate the eggs and raise
the chicks. After breeding,
both sexes spend up to
nine months at sea.

*Females have
pale golden
lines on
the back.*

*Red-brown
neck is deeper
in color in
females.*

*Feet are slightly
webbed to help with
swimming at sea.*

♀

Skuas and auks

Skuas are aggressive gull-like ocean birds, but auks—with their upright posture and black-and-white plumage—look more like penguins although they can fly. Auks use their wings to propel themselves underwater to catch fish, also like penguins.

Parasitic jaeger
Stercorarius parasiticus

There are two varieties of the parasitic jaeger—a pale-bellied form and a dark-bellied one. This coastal bird is a kleptoparasite: it gets some of its food by stealing it from other seabirds such as terns and puffins, mobbing them until they drop their catch of fish.

Dark cap

Central tail feathers are long and pointed.

This bird migrates from Arctic tundra to the tip of South America when not breeding.

Long, pointed wing

Atlantic puffin
Fratercula arctica

The Atlantic puffin only develops its brightly colored bill in the breeding season. At other times, its bill is grayer.

Rounded body

Common murre
Uria aalge

Nesting in colonies on steep coastal cliffs to avoid land predators, this bird lays a single egg on a bare ledge. Its young jump down into the water with their father before they can fly.

White underparts

Parakeet auklet
Aethia psittacula

The parakeet auklet breeds on rocky coasts of islands in the north Pacific, and parents may fly far out to sea to get food for their chicks. They dive to depths of 98½ ft (30 m) for their favorite prey—shrimplike animals—which they catch with their stubby, orange bill.

White plume behind whitish eye

Uniformly dark wing

Bright white underparts

Gulls

With their bold, noisy behavior, gulls are the shorebirds that are most likely to be seen and heard. They are not too fussy in how they get food—they fish for prey, take nestlings of other birds, and even steal from humans. Some species live inland, preferring freshwater lakes and marshes.

Bonaparte's gull
Chroicocephalus philadelphia

The Bonaparte's gull breeds far inland, nesting in spruce trees close to ponds and wetlands. It then migrates to spend winter along coasts and estuaries, where it may gather in flocks of thousands.

Underwing has black tips.

Head starts to turn white after breeding.

Black-legged kittiwake
Rissa tridactyla

Kittiwakes are named for the sound of their call. They stick closer to the coast than most other gulls, nesting in large clifftop colonies. These birds can often be seen fishing at sea.

Yellow bill

Herring gull
Larus argentatus

The most common gull in North America breeds almost anywhere—from Arctic tundra to the rooftops of city buildings. It takes advantage of our waste food by following the discarded catch of fishing boats or visiting garbage dumps inland.

Gray back

Black outer wing feathers

Pink, webbed feet paddle when swimming.

California gull
Larus californicus

This gull has a particular taste for insects—it has helped control swarms of locusts and grasshoppers. It also preys on worms, rodents, fishes, and birds' eggs, and even steals fruit from cherry farms.

Yellow, webbed feet

White underparts

Gray upperparts with black wing tips

Terns and skimmers

Terns are smaller, slimmer birds than gulls. They depend more on fishing in open water for food, and are often seen darting around in the skies above the surface. The subtropical skimmers use their strangely shaped bills to scoop fish.

Black tern
Chlidonias niger

This marsh-dwelling tern of inland freshwater has shorter wings than terns that fly at sea. It flutters over water to dip the surface for aquatic insects and small fishes. During winter, it migrates to the coast.

Gray upperparts

This tern sometimes uses old, abandoned muskrat burrows and grebe nests to raise its young.

Black summer plumage turns whitish in winter.

White patch under the tail

Common tern
Sterna hirundo

North America's most widespread tern breeds on inland marshes as well as along coastal beaches—sometimes in colonies of tens of thousands.

Black cap shrinks in winter.

Short tail streamers

Least tern
Sternula antillarum

The smallest beach-nesting tern regularly plunge-dives for fish in the sea from heights of up to 3 ft (10 m).

Yellow bill

Dark outer wing feathers

Caspian tern
Hydroprogne caspia

The chunky bill of the world's largest tern helps to catch bigger fish than other species. Sometimes it harasses other seabirds to steal their catch.

Dark tip on outer wing

Bill stays red all year.

Black skimmer
Rynchops niger

Having a longer lower bill than upper bill helps this bird skim for fish while flying forward just above the surface of the water.

Black upperparts

Orange-red and black bill

Seabirds, herons, and relatives

Some of the best adaptations for living at sea are seen in seabirds—soaring albatrosses use their sense of smell to find prey, while diving gannets plunge deep to get fish. Wetland herons and pelicans use their impressive bills for fishing.

PIGGYBACK CHICKS
Many waterbird parents, such as the common loon, carry their chicks on their back—to keep them warm and protect them from predators.

Loons

The feet of these birds are set so far back on their body that they can hardly stand upright on land, so they push forward on their bellies. In water, the feet turn into powerful paddles for swimming.

Common loon
Gavia immer

Shiny, green head and neck

Like other loon species, the common loon breeds on cold northern lakes, where its eerie wailing call can be heard over great distances. It spends the winter along coastlines farther south—around rocky shores and sheltered bays.

The common loon can dive down to 230 ft (70 m) in the deepest lakes.

Pacific loon
Gavia pacifica

North America's most abundant species of loon is most likely to be seen when it migrates along the Pacific coast, including California.

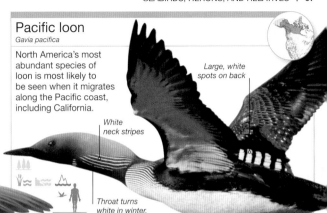

Large, white spots on back

White neck stripes

Throat turns white in winter.

Red-throated loon
Gavia stellata

Head is usually held tilted upward.

Brown wings and back

Red-brown throat patch

The smallest loon builds its nest—a mound of wet vegetation—on wetlands and ponds of Arctic moorland, but parents fly to the coast to catch cod, herring, and other sea fishes to feed their chicks.

Albatrosses, petrels, and shearwaters

No birds spend as much time out on the open ocean as albatrosses and their relatives, which are masters of the air. Their keen sense of smell helps them sniff out squid and fish.

Black-footed albatross

Phoebastria nigripes

For most of the year, the black-footed albatross flies far from land—but each winter, adult pairs (with a male and a female) return to the Hawaiian Islands to raise a single chick.

White patch under the tail

Pale stripe below eye

Black-footed albatrosses may live more than 40 years.

Dark gray plumage

Long wings spanning up to 6½ ft (2.1 m) help the albatross soar effortlessly on strong ocean winds.

Wilson's storm-petrel

Oceanites oceanicus

Sparrow-sized petrels flutter their wings and dip their tiny webbed feet in the water as they pluck small fish and shrimp from the surface.

Tubelike nostrils on beak

Northern fulmar

Fulmarus glacialis

Looking more like a gull than an albatross relative, the northern fulmar nests in huge colonies on cliffs.

Thick, hooked bill

Pale patch on wing

Sooty shearwater

Ardenna grisea

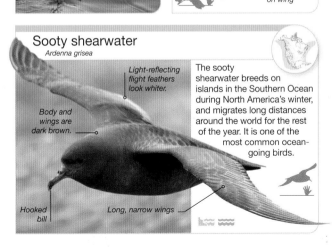

Light-reflecting flight feathers look whiter.

Body and wings are dark brown.

The sooty shearwater breeds on islands in the Southern Ocean during North America's winter, and migrates long distances around the world for the rest of the year. It is one of the most common ocean-going birds.

Hooked bill

Long, narrow wings

Frigatebirds, gannets, and cormorants

Gannets dive deep from a great height. But their relatives are less waterproof—frigatebirds stick near the surface and cormorants must dry out after taking a dip. They all have webbed feet.

Magnificent frigatebird
Fregata magnificens

Long wings take frigatebirds far out to sea. When not catching flying fish, they are pirates—harassing other seabirds to steal their catch.

♂

Black plumage

Red throat pouch in males

A frigatebird's absorbent feathers can make it drown if it spends too much time in water.

Northern gannet
Morus bassanus

Yellowish head

Sharp edge of beak grips fish.

All four toes on the webbed feet are linked by skin.

By pulling its wings back and diving downward, an airborne gannet plunges into the sea to catch fish and squid.

Anhinga
Anhinga anhinga

♂

Silver-white markings on wings

Black neck in males, pale brown in females

Ridged tail

The anhinga fishes in tropical lakes and rivers. Like its cormorant relatives, it then stretches its wings out to dry them in the sun.

Double-crested cormorant
Nannopterum auritum

Unlike plunge-diving gannets, cormorants dive from the water surface—but then use their feet like paddles to chase fish underwater. Thousands of double-crested cormorants may work together to force schools of fish into tight bunches, making them easier to catch. Those found on the Pacific have crests of white feathers.

Shiny dark green and lavender body

Storks and pelicans

Birds with the biggest bills can generally get the biggest meals. Long-legged storks use their bill to feel for prey, which are grabbed with a snap, while pelican bills have a pouch that nets lots of fish at once.

FOCUS ON...
FISHING
Pelicans have the biggest bills of any bird—but use them in two very different fishing techniques.

▲ The brown pelican plunge-dives for fish in coastal waters.

▲ The American white pelican swims on lakes, scooping fish with its bill.

Wood stork
Mycteria americana

North America's only species of stork is a large bird of warm wetlands, such as the Everglades. Here, it hunts freshwater prey that includes catfishes, snakes, and even baby alligators.

Black flight feathers on white wing

Bare black skin on head and neck

Unwebbed toes turn pink during the breeding season.

The wood stork stirs mud with its feet to flush out prey.

Brown pelican
Pelecanus occidentalis

Adults have mainly brown plumage.

Unlike white pelicans of inland freshwater, the brown pelican is only found on seawater—and relies on schools of anchovies and sardines for most of its food. It often perches around harbors, waiting for scraps from people fishing.

Hook at tip of bill helps grip fish.

As in other pelicans, all four toes are connected by webbing.

Brown neck turns white outside the breeding season.

American white pelican
Pelecanus erythrorhynchos

The American white pelican fishes mainly in freshwater areas but may wander to the coast. Groups often work together to herd fish into tighter schools that are easier to scoop up.

A flat horn grows on the upper bill in the breeding season.

Black flight feathers on white wing

Yellow-orange legs

Brown pelicans can start their dive from up to

66 ft (20 m)

in the air

PLUNGE-DIVER
At the moment of impact, plunge-diving brown pelicans hold their large wings and feet back to cut through the water, before opening their bill to scoop fish into their pouch.

Bitterns, herons, egrets, and ibises

Bitterns, herons, and egrets are expert fishers that can stand perfectly still and strike with a lightning-fast stab of the bill. Ibises need less patience as they probe the mud for slow animal prey.

American bittern
Botaurus lentiginosus

The American bittern is a secretive bird. Its streaky brown plumage blends perfectly into reedy vegetation, so it is more likely to be heard than seen. Its low, booming *dunk-a-doo* call can carry for miles.

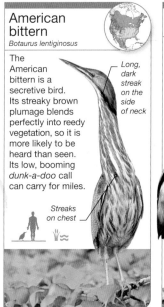

Long, dark streak on the side of neck

Streaks on chest

Least bittern
Ixobrychus exilis

The smallest member of the heron family clambers over vegetation with its big, clawed feet. It can easily slip through little gaps in search of small fishes and insects.

Long, yellow bill

Black cap in males, brown in females

White streaks on belly

♂

Great blue heron
Ardea herodias

The legs of this large, conspicuous heron are long enough to wade deeper for fish than its cousins. It nests in large treetop colonies—sometimes far from water.

Striped crown

Crest feathers are not always raised and visible.

Long, gray neck

Shaggy plumage

Tricolored heron
Egretta tricolor

Named for the many colours on its plumage, this bird is more likely to be found on coastal waters than other herons.

Dark neck contrasts with white belly.

Blue bill

Snowy egret
Egretta thula

This bird was once hunted for its white plumes, which were used to decorate hats. Its numbers have now recovered.

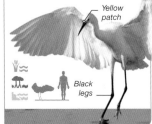

Yellow patch

Black legs

Green heron
Butorides virescens

In parts of its range, the green heron has learned to use bait to help catch prey—it lays insects or even stolen crusts of bread in shallow water, then waits for a fish to come within striking distance.

Greenish-black crown

Prominent yellow eyes

Long feathers on the back

Brown neck and sides

Cream streak stretches from throat to belly.

By using bait, the green heron is one of the few tool-using birds in the world.

Orange legs and feet

Black-crowned night-heron
Nycticorax nycticorax

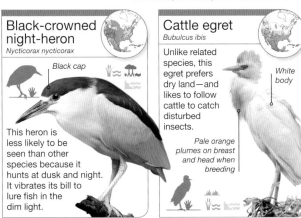

Black cap

This heron is less likely to be seen than other species because it hunts at dusk and night. It vibrates its bill to lure fish in the dim light.

Cattle egret
Bubulcus ibis

Unlike related species, this egret prefers dry land—and likes to follow cattle to catch disturbed insects.

White body

Pale orange plumes on breast and head when breeding

White ibis
Eudocimus albus

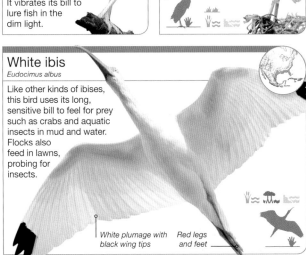

Like other kinds of ibises, this bird uses its long, sensitive bill to feel for prey such as crabs and aquatic insects in mud and water. Flocks also feed in lawns, probing for insects.

White plumage with black wing tips

Red legs and feet

Vultures, hawks, eagles, and owls

Most birds of prey have weapons—a hooked bill and talons—that help them kill for their meal. They also rely on super senses to catch their target—superb vision and sharp hearing to watch and listen for movement. Others, such as vultures, scavenge dead animals for their food—a few even guided by smell.

FISH CATCHER
Many eagles have thickly feathered legs, but those of a bald eagle are bare— making it easier for them to grab fish from water.

American vultures and osprey

Vultures are the biggest flying scavengers, often soaring high over dry land to find dead animals to eat. In contrast, the osprey is an expert fisher that always lives near water.

Turkey vulture
Cathartes aura

Unusually for birds, this vulture has a good sense of smell—which it uses to locate carcasses of dead animals while flying high above the ground. It rarely kills to eat.

Pink, warty skin on head

Black vultures often follow turkey vultures to find food.

Feet have a very short hind toe, as in all American vultures.

Brownish-black plumage

Black vulture
Coragyps atratus

This scavenger searches places that are likely to have dead meat, such as roadsides and garbage dumps. But it can also hunt prey, such as baby birds and reptiles.

Black feathers

California condor
Gymnogyps californianus

ENDANGERED

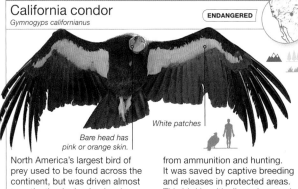

Bare head has pink or orange skin.

White patches

North America's largest bird of prey used to be found across the continent, but was driven almost to extinction by lead poisoning from ammunition and hunting. It was saved by captive breeding and releases in protected areas. This bird is critically endangered.

Osprey
Pandion haliaetus

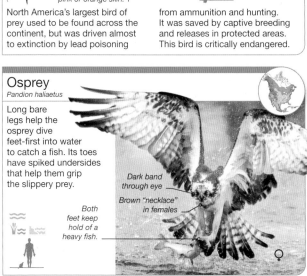

Long bare legs help the osprey dive feet-first into water to catch a fish. Its toes have spiked undersides that help them grip the slippery prey.

Dark band through eye

Brown "necklace" in females

Both feet keep hold of a heavy fish.

♀

Kites, eagles, hawks, and harriers

Some of these day-flying raptors, or birds of prey, are specialized to hunt particular types of animals, but all are meat-eaters—with excellent eyesight, hooked bills, and sharp talons on their feet.

FOCUS ON... **HUNTING**

Raptors have great weapons to attack prey on a hunt.

▲ Most eagles and hawks kill prey with their strong stabbing talons.

▲ A snail kite's bill has an extra-long hook to pull snails from shells.

White-tailed kite
Elanus leucurus

By hovering in the air over the ground, a white-tailed kite can keep scanning for its favorite prey—scurrying mice and other rodents. It can also snatch other small birds in flight.

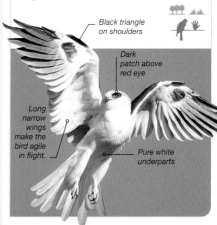

Black triangle on shoulders

Dark patch above red eye

Long narrow wings make the bird agile in flight.

Pure white underparts

Golden eagle
Aquila chrysaetos

North America's largest hunting bird of prey can kill animals as big as young deer. It swoops down to strike a blow with its taloned feet.

Dark brown body, usually pale behind the neck

Northern harrier
Circus hudsonius

Hunting in open country, the northern harrier flies low over the ground—sometimes gliding—and listens for prey, such as rodents and birds.

Brown feathers in females, gray in males

♀

Cooper's hawk
Accipiter cooperii

This long-tailed forest hawk catches most of its prey on the ground near woodland edges or clearings, moving expertly around trees.

Dark bands on gray tail, which has a rounded tip.

Northern goshawk
Accipiter gentilis

The northern goshawk watches from a hidden perch—before darting out to grab squirrels, grouse, or other woodland prey.

Distinct white line over eye

Red-tailed hawk

Buteo jamaicensis

The most common bird of prey in North America, the red-tailed hawk is at home wherever it can hunt in open countryside. It has been spreading farther across the continent as forests have been cut down to make way for fields and pasture.

Dark wingtips

Large eyes help spot prey, such as mice, easily.

Reddish-brown tail

A red-tailed hawk can dive at a top speed of 120 mph (193 kph) when seeking prey.

Reddish-brown streaks on body, and brown or white underparts

Bald eagle
Haliaeetus leucocephalus

Hooked bill

Chocolate-brown wings and body

Adults have white feathers on the head.

Yellow legs and feet

Wedge-shaped white tail

The national emblem of the US, this large sea eagle catches fish and waterbirds. But in winter, it can also be found far from water, where it relies more on catching mammals or scavenging for dead animals.

Mississippi kite
Ictinia mississippiensis

A common sight in farmland or even towns, the Mississippi kite mainly hunts large insects, such as cicadas and dragonflies.

Dark gray wings

Snail kite
Rostrhamus sociabilis

Seen mainly in south Florida, this bird of prey flies low to grab aquatic snails from shallow water, then perches to use its hooked bill for pulling out their flesh.

Females are brown, males are gray

♀

Owls

Most types of owls are superbly equipped to hunt prey at night or twilight. Their sensitive ears can hear the slightest movement of prey, while their big eyes work well in low-level moonlight. Owls can also swoop down silently to catch prey by surprise.

Barn owl
Tyto alba

The barn owl's pale color and loud shrieking call make it hard to miss at night. Its hearing is so sensitive that it can pinpoint the position of prey in complete darkness.

Heart-shaped facial disk

Eastern screech-owl
Megascops asio

Like other owls, this small hunter catches prey—anything from insects to rodents—with its feet, sometimes running after the target.

Small, feathery ear tufts

Black rim on facial disk

White markings on inner wing feathers

FOCUS ON...
SENSING PREY

Special adaptations help owls locate their prey and fly without being heard by their target.

▲ A disk-shaped face helps collect the faintest sounds made by moving prey, which are channeled toward each ear.

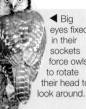

◀ Big eyes fixed in their sockets force owls to rotate their head to look around.

Great horned owl

Bubo virginianus

Broad wings

Prominent yellow eyes

White throat

The largest owl in North America is powerful enough to kill prey the size of rabbits and herons. Like other owls, it swallows smaller animals whole, but will tear bigger prey to pieces.

Snowy owl

Bubo scandiacus

A bird of the treeless Arctic tundra, the snowy owl nests on the ground. It hunts lemmings, which it catches by listening for them burrowing under the snow.

Females have barred underparts, males are sometimes pure white beneath

White face in both sexes

Pure white under the wing

♀

A pair of young burrowing owls peer out from their underground nest—usually a unused burrow of another animal, such as a ground squirrel. Rarely, parents will excavate holes—digging with their bill and kicking the soil backward.

Unlike most owls, burrowing owls are active

during the day,

hopping and running to catch big insects and small rodents

Northern hawk owl
Surnia ulula

This owl nests in tree holes in the cold northern coniferous forests. It stores frozen mice in hollow trees for future meals.

White face with black markings

Barred underparts with long tail

Long-eared owl
Asio otus

Dark markings on body

The long-eared owl has long ear tufts that can be folded down. At home in thick forests, it listens for prey while flying under the canopy—sometimes hovering to focus on a target. If it catches a vole, it deals a death blow with a swift bite to the back of the rodent's head.

Streaked underparts

Great gray owl
Strix nebulosa

The great gray owl listens for hidden rodents under the snow in coniferous forests before diving feet first into the snow to catch a meal.

Large facial disk with white crescents

Long, barred, mottled gray wings

Boreal owl
Aegolius funereus

The boreal owl lives so far north that when the summer Arctic sun stays above the horizon and doesn't set, it is forced to hunt in daylight. It then combines good vision with acute hearing to locate prey.

Brown back and tail have white spots.

Whitish belly

Kingfishers, woodpeckers, and falcons

These birds live in habitats as varied as dense forest, open prairies, and wetland, and have different ways of finding their animal food. Kingfishers get their prey by diving into water, woodpeckers by probing tree trunks, and falcons by snatching flying targets in the sky. Kingfishers and woodpeckers are hole-nesters, but many falcons are happier on exposed ledges.

FAST FALCON
Peregrine falcons prey on other flying birds, such as pigeons, by dive-bombing them—swooping down at record-breaking speed.

Kingfishers and woodpeckers

These birds have strong pointed bills, but they use them in different ways. Kingfishers grab fish, while woodpeckers chisel trees to uncover insect prey and hammer to make nest holes or be heard.

Belted kingfisher
Megaceryle alcyon

Like other kingfishers, this bird catches a fish by plunge-diving straight toward its prey. Sometimes it hovers in the air to help focus on its target before doing so.

Only females have a brown breast band.

The sharp edges of the bill help it grip slippery fish.

♀

Red-headed woodpecker
Melanerpes erythrocephalus

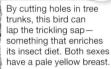

As well as eating seeds and nuts, this bird is also an expert at catching insects on the wing—unusual behavior for woodpeckers.

Black upperparts with white wing feathers

Red-bellied woodpecker
Melanerpes carolinus

♂

Like many other woodpeckers, the sexes of this species have different head markings. The males have more red on their crown than females.

Yellow-bellied sapsucker
Sphyrapicus varius

By cutting holes in tree trunks, this bird can lap the trickling sap—something that enriches its insect diet. Both sexes have a pale yellow breast.

Red chin in males, white in females

♂

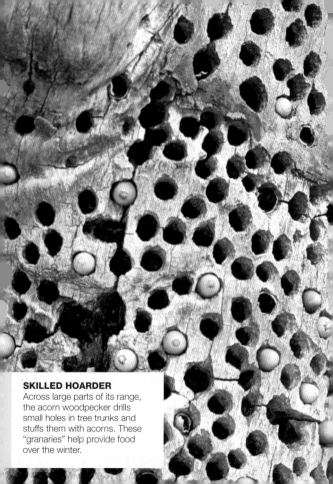

SKILLED HOARDER
Across large parts of its range, the acorn woodpecker drills small holes in tree trunks and stuffs them with acorns. These "granaries" help provide food over the winter.

Granaries are used from year to year and trees can end up with

50,000 holes

drilled in their sides

American three-toed woodpecker
Picoides dorsalis

This little woodpecker breeds farther north than any other species of woodpecker—in tall Canadian conifer forests, where it searches the trunks for bark beetles, its favorite food. Males have a yellow forehead and females have a black-and-white crown.

Black-and-white bars on back

Downy woodpecker
Dryobates pubescens

Named for the soft white feathers on its back, the smallest woodpecker in North America is often seen feeding with other small birds, such as tits. It visits garden feeders in winter. Only males have a red head patch.

Northern flicker
Colaptes auratus

The northern flicker flashes its red underwings when courting or defending territory. The colors are brighter in the males—they have a more prominent red or black "mustache."

Pileated woodpecker

Dryocopus pileatus

Like other woodpeckers, this bird uses its bill to excavate a hole in the wood of a tree to make a nest. Male and female share the task—and both feed the chicks.

Bright red crest in both sexes

Chicks beg for food with open bills.

Red "mustache" and forehead in males, black in females

♂

It can take about six weeks for a pair of pileated woodpeckers to dig a nest hole.

White patch on wings

Caracaras and falcons

Although they look like hawks, falcons are more closely related to parrots. They fly fast when hunting, and a sharp notch in their bill helps them kill with a bite. Their cousins, the caracaras, are less fussy, and may eat dead animals or fruit.

Crested caracara
Caracara plancus

The crested caracara gets its name from its chattering call. This bird hunts, but also scavenges or even steals. It chases turkey vultures and black vultures in flight to make them drop their food.

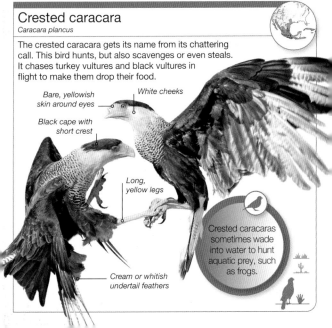

Bare, yellowish skin around eyes

White cheeks

Black cape with short crest

Long, yellow legs

Cream or whitish undertail feathers

Crested caracaras sometimes wade into water to hunt aquatic prey, such as frogs.

Prairie falcon
Falco mexicanus

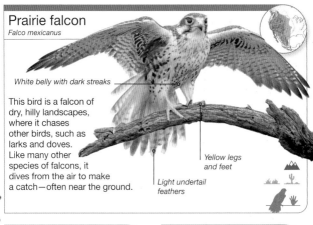

White belly with dark streaks

This bird is a falcon of dry, hilly landscapes, where it chases other birds, such as larks and doves. Like many other species of falcons, it dives from the air to make a catch—often near the ground.

Yellow legs and feet

Light undertail feathers

Merlin
Falco columbarius

The merlin has a fast, dashing flight and is expert at catching small prey, such as birds, bats, and dragonflies, on the wing.

Brown upperparts in females

Streaked underparts

Pointed wings beat fast.

American kestrel
Falco sparverius

When perched or hovering high above the ground, this bird searches for a target—usually a big insect or mouse—before swooping down to catch it.

Blue on wings in males

Passerines

Nearly two-thirds of all bird species are passerines. They are sometimes called "perching birds" because of the way their toes can firmly grip a branch—usually with three pointing forward and one back. Most are accomplished songbirds too, thanks to a special "song box" at the base of their windpipe.

COMMON CARDINAL
Passerines include some of the most abundant and successful bird species. The northern cardinal is found in forests, grassland, and deserts.

FOCUS ON...
SPOT THE DIFFERENCE

Some tyrants look so similar that habitat and sounds are needed to tell them apart.

Tyrants

With their broad pointed bills and agile movements, tyrants are expert flycatchers. They usually flit from their perch to catch insects on the wing, or swoop down to grab them from the ground.

▲ The Acadian flycatcher breeds in swampy woods and has a piping *pweet* call.

▲ The willow flycatcher breeds in wet shrubby habitats and its *fitz-bew* call sounds more like a sneeze.

Scissor-tailed flycatcher
Tyrannus forficatus

With its long trailing tail feathers, this bird makes a lovely sight as it flies gracefully upwards to chase insects in flight. Its courtship display is impressive too – as it zigzags through the air to impress a mate.

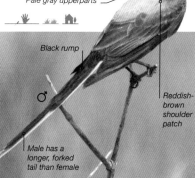

Pale gray upperparts

Black rump

♂

Reddish-brown shoulder patch

Male has a longer, forked tail than female

Eastern kingbird
Tyrannus tyrannus

Kingbirds give tyrant flycatchers their name: the eastern kingbird defends its nest and territory by aggressively driving other birds away.

White tail tip

Eastern phoebe
Sayornis phoebe

Phoebes get their name from their *fee-bee* song. The eastern phoebe's habit of nesting under bridges has helped it spread in parts of North America.

Olive breast

Vermilion flycatcher
Pyrocephalus rubinus

The striking vermilion flycatcher is a bird of the drier southwestern states, where it often perches in the open, wagging its tail up and down. Only males are red – females are streaky brown.

Male has a black face mask.

Brownish black wings

Orange-red breast in males, white in females

♂

Vireos and shrikes

The birds of this group have slightly oversized bills compared with other similar-sized birds. Vireos use theirs for plucking insects and berries from branches, but shrikes are more like mini-falcons—attacking prey up to the size of lizards and mice.

Red-eyed vireo
Vireo olivaceus

Red eyes with black head stripes

Olive upperparts

Bluish legs and feet

One of the most common of North America's woodland birds, the red-eyed vireo is a summer visitor, spending the winter in the Amazon basin. It is an enthusiastic singer—right through the day and even sometimes on migration.

Warbling vireo
Vireo gilvus

The warbling vireo has a sweeter, more warbling song than the monotonous call of the red-eyed vireo, but it is just as persistent. Males may keep singing even when sitting on eggs in the nest.

White eyebrow

Grayish-green upperparts

Short tail

Blue-headed vireo
Vireo solitarius

More common in coniferous forests than other vireos, the blue-headed vireo flits around the middle-levels of trees, where—like its cousins—it often catches insects on the wing.

A male's sweet song can have 20 different phrases, separated by brief pauses.

White "spectacles" around eyes

Bright greenish sides

Loggerhead shrike
Lanius ludovicianus

Like other shrikes, this bird has a habit of impaling prey—including smaller birds—on thorns or barbed wire. These gruesome larders mean the shrike does not have to eat all its meat at once. The sharp notch in this predator's hooked bill is enough to cut through its prey's flesh and bone.

Black face mask

Striking black-and-white plumage

Rounded tail with white edges

Crows, jays, and magpies

The crow family includes intelligent birds that use brainpower to solve ways of getting food or an impressive memory to remember where they have stored it. Most have harsh cawing voices but some are also able to mimic sounds.

Black-billed magpie
Pica hudsonia

The black-billed magpie often sticks close to other animals—as a way of getting a free meal. It takes insect prey from cow pats, and even sneaks in to grab meat from kills left by hunting wolves.

Long, tapering tail

Prominent white shoulders

Dark parts of the plumage have a bluish-metallic shine.

Magpies may pluck blood-sucking ticks from the backs of moose.

Common raven
Corvus corax

The world's biggest passerine is a scavenger as well as an expert hunter of small animals, such as rodents and nestlings of other birds.

Black plumage with purple shine

Thick bill

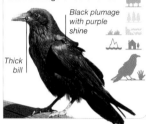

Canada jay
Perisoreus canadensis

A bird of the northern forests, the Canada jay survives the coldest months on food that it stored under bark the previous summer.

Pale gray plumage

Long tail

Blue jay
Cyanocitta cristata

A familiar woodland and garden bird, the blue jay has a taste for seasonal acorns and beechmast—which it stores for the winter.

The crest is raised when the bird is excited or aggressive.

White patches on blue wings

Tits, larks, and swallows

Acrobatic little woodland birds, tits are common visitors to garden feeders. Larks prefer open habitats and spend much of their time on the ground, while swallows and martins are masters of the skies—swooping to catch flying insects on the wing.

Tufted titmouse

Baeolophus bicolor

In typical tit fashion, this bird jumps through the branches, picking off insects and sometimes hanging upside-down to reach them. It also holds acorns and other nuts with its feet while hammering them to pieces with its bill.

Dark gray tufts

Prominent orange sides

Gray-black feet and legs

Black-capped chickadee

Poecile atricapillus

Black cap and chin contrast with white cheeks.

White edges on tail

White underparts tinged with brown

Among lots of different sounds, the *chick-a-dee* call of this bird is especially memorable, and gives the bird its name. Like other tits, it nests in tree holes—and will often take advantage of nest boxes.

Horned lark
Eremophila alpestris

The only species of lark found in North America nests in tufts of grass on open ground and lives in lots of barren landscapes—from mountains to seashores. It can raise or lower the hornlike tufts of feathers on its head.

Males have a deeper breast band than females.

Streaked, reddish-brown upperparts

The female digs a shallow depression in the ground for her nest, using her bill and feet.

♂

Barn swallow
Hirundo rustica

Before there were houses, the barn swallow nested in caves. But now it almost always chooses the eaves of buildings or under bridges.

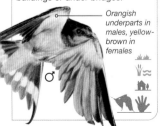

Orangish underparts in males, yellow-brown in females

♂

Purple martin
Progne subis

Like the barn swallow, the purple martin migrates to tropical South America during winter, when supplies of flying insect food farther north decline.

Female has a grayish throat and belly but males are blue-black all over.

♀

Kinglets, waxwings, and relatives

Bushtits and kinglets are among the smallest insect-eating birds in North America—only slightly bigger than hummingbirds. Waxwings are starling-sized birds that rely more on sweet berries for their food.

Bushtit
Psaltriparus minimus

Bushtits sometimes huddle together in groups inside their hanging pouch-shaped nests at night to keep warm. Like true tits, this tiny bird hops along branches—sometimes upside-down—to grab insects and spiders.

Long tail

Females have paler eyes than males.

♀

Gray plumage

Older youngsters sometimes help their parents to raise their next brood.

Ruby-crowned kinglet
Corthylio calendula

Only males have a red crest.

White eye ring

♂

Olive-green plumage

Like some other tiny birds, the ruby-crowned kinglet uses sticky spider webs to help hold its nest together. This bird produces more eggs than most other small birds.

Cedar waxwing
Bombycilla cedrorum

Waxwings get their name from the unique red waxy tips of their wing's flight feathers. Large winter flocks of cedar waxwings gather to feed on cedar berries and other fruit—and scatter the seeds in their droppings.

Black mask edged with white

Red waxy tips

Distinct yellow tail tip

Nuthatches, wrens, and relatives

Nuthatches and creepers are tree-climbers—they grip tree trunks with their strong feet when searching for food. Wrens and gnatcatchers are more likely to flit about among branches.

Red-breasted nuthatch
Sitta canadensis

Acrobatic nuthatches can climb upward and downward on a trunk. These birds store insects and seeds when they are plentiful, hiding them in bark crevices to use in the winter.

Black crown in males, gray in females

♂

Brown creeper
Certhia americana

Using its stiff tail as a prop, this insect-eater climbs up a trunk, but it can't descend head first, so it hops backward or flies down. It uses its thin bill to pull insects from the bark.

White streaks in brown plumage

Forked tail

Blue-gray gnatcatcher
Polioptila caerulea

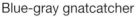

Most species of gnatcatchers live in tropical America, but this is the only one to reach into the US. Despite its name, this bird eats lots of kinds of insects and spiders—but has no particular taste for gnats.

White eye-ring

♂

Blue-gray upperparts in males, pale gray in females

White outer tail feathers

Flicking tail may help flush out insects from foliage.

Winter wren
Troglodytes hiemalis

The winter wren has one of the loudest songs for a bird of its tiny size. It is usually seen flitting among thickets close to the forest floor.

Slightly paler underparts

Short tail is typically held upright.

Brown plumage has darker barred markings.

Mockingbirds, thrashers, and dippers

These birds of open habitats are best known for their song—and some are even impressive mimics. Dippers, of mountain streams, sing loudly too, over the sound of running water.

Northern mockingbird
Mimus polyglottos

The northern mockingbird incorporates calls of other birds into its songs to make its vocals as impressive as possible. It develops more different songs as it gets older and gets experienced—and both sexes sing.

An older male mockingbird may end up with more than 150 songs.

Long tail with white feathers

Large white patch near "shoulder" of wing

Brown thrasher
Toxostoma rufum

As vocal as a mockingbird, the brown thrasher spends much of its time on the ground, where it searches for insect prey by flipping through leaf litter—and takes advantage of seasonal falls of fruit and nuts.

Yellow eye

Reddish-brown upperparts

Long, brown tail

Bold black streaks on underparts

Gray catbird
Dumetella carolinensis

This bird gets its name from its mewing call, but can also use its dual-purpose song box to sing two songs at the same time.

Gray upperparts

Red undertail feathers

American dipper
Cinclus mexicanus

Streamside dippers are the only passerine birds that dive into water, where they catch aquatic insects. They even walk on the streambed.

White eyelid

Bluebirds, thrushes, and pipits

Bluebirds, thrushes, and their relatives spend much time hopping about on the ground in woodland and gardens. Pipits are birds of open habitats.

Eastern bluebird
Sialia sialis

The eastern bluebird often lives and nests close to humans, and its bold antics makes it an easy bird to watch and study. It readily uses nest boxes.

Reddish-brown underparts in males, whiter underparts in females

Blue wings in both sexes

♂

An eastern bluebird makes a *churr-wi* or *churr-li* note, which may sound like "truly."

Townsend's solitaire
Myadestes townsendi

In winter, this bird of mountain forests and woodland comes down to warmer valleys to find plenty of winter berries.

White eye-ring

Veery
Catharus fuscescens

After breeding in wet, swampy forests in North America, this thrush then migrates south to spend winter in South America, stopping off in the Amazon basin.

Cinnamon upperparts

Swainson's thrush
Catharus ustulatus

This bird's song sounds like a flute but it lives and sings in thick forest. Like other thrushes, it flips through leaf litter to search for food, but also spends lots of time in the high canopy.

Buffy "spectacles"

Olive-brown upperparts

White belly with dark brown spots

A brown-headed
cowbird can lay up to

40 eggs

each breeding season—always in the
nests of other bird species

ODD ONE OUT
A speckled egg of a brown-headed cowbird laid in the nest of an eastern bluebird looks nothing like the blue eggs of the rightful owner. But there is a high chance that the parent bluebird will not notice – and so will raise the cowbird chick as its own.

Wood thrush
Hylocichla mustelina

The wood thrush prefers the cover of forest in summer—where it nests in the fork of a tree. In fall, it wanders into clearings, searching for fruit.

Brownish back contrasts with rusty head

White underparts with bold black spots

Brown tail

Pinkish legs and toes

American robin
Turdus migratorius

♀

A familiar garden bird, the American robin is found wherever there are insects, worms, and fruit for eating, and trees for nesting.

Chicks beg for food.

Paler underparts in females

Varied thrush
Ixoreus naevius

Like other thrushes, this bird builds a cup-shaped nest from grass and moss. But it is fussy with habitat—breeding in dark, wet coniferous forest.

In winter, the varied thrush may wander into parks and gardens.

Black chest band in males, gray in females

Bold black and orange-brown markings

♂

American pipit
Anthus rubescens

The American pipit is the only species of pipit found in North America. Like other pipits in Europe or Asia, this ground-nesting bird catches insects in open country.

Tail may be bobbed frequently.

Pale stripe above eye

White outer tail feathers

Pale brown underparts with darker streaks

This bird may be getting ready to fly!

Finches and relatives

Finches are seed-eaters—and they are well adapted for the task. Their bills are strong enough to smash the outer casing of seeds to reach the edible flesh inside.

House finch
Haemorhous mexicanus

Like other finches, parent birds feed seeds and fruit to their chicks by spewing up partially digested food from their gut. The male's red color comes from pigments that are found in its diet.

Brick-red bib and head

Red plumage in males, streaked brown plumage in females

Brown wings and back

Belly fades to pink and white, streaked with brown

♂

Red crossbill
Loxia curvirostra

The upper and lower bill of this bird cross over at the tips. This unusual feature helps it pull seeds from the cones of pines and other conifer trees.

Greenish-brown plumage in females, red in males

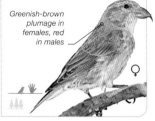

♀

American goldfinch
Spinus tristis

This common garden bird has a sharply pointed bill so it can extract seeds from the heads of thistles, teasels, and dandelions.

Black crown

Breeding males are bright yellow, females are dull yellow

♂

Pine grosbeak
Pinicola enucleator

A finch of cold northern forests, the pine grosbeak may gather in winter flocks with other finches, such as crossbills.

Females are gray or greenish, males are red

Pale patch under eye

♀

Common redpoll
Acanthis flammea

This bird lives in more open country than other kinds of finches. It moves south every few years when conifer seed crops are scarce further north.

Males have a rosy-red breast.

 ♂

Longspurs, buntings, and sparrows

These birds have the seed-cracking bills of finches, but lack their bright colours. They are patterned with browns, greys, black, and white instead. Most are found in open habitats.

FOCUS ON...
PLUMAGE

Seasonal molts mean that the colours of some species change a lot through the year.

▶ A breeding male snow bunting is mostly white, which camouflages it against the Arctic snow.

▶ Both sexes turn brown when migrating south during the winter.

Lapland longspur
Calcarius lapponicus

Named for its long, spurlike hind claws, the Lapland longspur breeds further north than almost any other small bird – nesting on the frozen Arctic ground, where only rocks and small shrubs provide shelter.

Chestnut neck and black face in breeding males

♂

White underparts

Grasshopper sparrow
Ammodramus savannarum

This sparrow has a trilling, grasshopper-like song, but also has a taste for these insects, hopping about the ground to search for food.

Lark bunting
Calamospiza melanocorys

The lark bunting relies more on insects in summer and seeds in winter – wandering the plains in search of the best supply.

Breeding males are black and white.

♂

Chipping sparrow
Spizella passerina

The trilling song of this sparrow is often heard from a tree or rooftop. It prefers more wooded habitat than most other kinds of sparrows, and it is a common summer visitor of towns and gardens.

Chestnut-brown crown

Black eyeline runs through the eye.

Plain unstreaked breast

Dark-eyed junco
Junco hyemalis

One of the most common of North American birds, the dark-eyed junco is tame and often visits feeders—especially during the winter, when it gathers in large flocks.

Gray back in males, brown in females

White outer tail feathers can be seen when it flies.

♂

White belly

White-crowned sparrow
Zonotrichia leucophrys

Often seen feeding on the ground with other sparrows and juncos, this bird is adaptable across much of its huge range—from tundra to prairie and mountains.

Black-and-white head pattern

White band on brown wing

In different parts of its range, this sparrow sings with distinct dialects.

Song sparrow
Melospiza melodia

Male song sparrows sing their short, cheerful song as a way of defending their territory. It can be heard throughout the year but especially during the breeding season. This is a variable species—different races found across North America have different color patterns and songs.

Dark "mustache" next to white throat

Dark spot in the center of the breast

Spotted towhee
Pipilo maculatus

The spotted towhee prefers to keep to the cover of thickets, where it scratches for insects and seeds among the leaf litter. This sparrow has a catlike mewing call.

Black head in males, browner in females

♂

Chestnut-brown sides

White underparts

Blackbirds and relatives

As well as grackles and blackbirds, this family includes brightly coloured orioles. Some birds in this group have unusual breeding habits—some nest in colonies, while others, such as the brown-headed cowbird, lay eggs in nests that are not their own!

Yellow-breasted chat
Icteria virens

Despite its bright yellow color, this secretive bird usually likes to stick to the cover of dense vegetation and is more often heard than seen. It has a loud whistling or rattling call. Male chats have a bouncing courtship flight, with legs dangling down, to impress females.

Gray face patch in females, black in males

Olive-green wings

Blackish legs and feet

Both sexes have a yellow throat and chest.

♀

Yellow-headed blackbird
Xanthocephalus xanthocephalus

This bird nests in large marshland colonies, with hundreds of nests attached to reeds over the water. Males mate with several females and help them defend the nests and feed the chicks.

Yellow and black feathers in males, browner in females

♂

Long tail

Bobolink
Dolichonyx oryzivorus

The bobolink has a long migration—after breeding on meadows in North America, it overwinters in South American marshes.

Black and white flight feathers in males, brownish in females

♂

Pointed tail feathers

Eastern meadowlark
Sturnella magna

Female meadowlarks build an impressive ground nest— it is covered by a grassy dome and sometimes has a yard-long entrance tunnel.

Yellow belly

Orchard oriole
Icterus spurius

Like other American orioles, this bird builds a hanging nest that resembles a basket, carefully woven from grass. Younger birds may help a pair raise their chicks.

♂

Black tail

Male is black and chestnut, female is yellow

Baltimore oriole
Icterus galbula

A male Baltimore oriole takes two years to turn black and orange—he is duller and yellower, like the female, in his first year.

White edges on wings

♂

Red-winged blackbird
Agelaius phoeniceus

Males of this species have more female mates than any other bird—up to 15 recorded. The brown females build their nests alone.

♂

Brown-headed cowbird
Molothrus ater

Cowbirds lay their eggs in the nests of other birds; they do not raise their own chicks. They target the nests of many birds, including tyrants, vireos, warblers, and sparrows.

Dark brown head and throat

♂

Male has a black body, female is all brown

Brown-headed cowbird chicks are known to be raised by as many as 144 different species.

Common grackle
Quiscalus quiscula

The common grackle's large, cup-shaped nest is made from grass leaves, sometimes paper and string, and sealed with mud. Unlike many birds, if it spots a rogue cowbird egg in its nest, it throws the egg out.

Shiny blue-black plumage

♂

Male grackles have a longer tail than females.

Wood warblers

More than 50 species of American warblers spend their summers in North America before overwintering in the tropics farther south. Most live in forests, but others prefer more open habitats and marshland.

Ovenbird
Seiurus aurocapilla

The ovenbird is a mainly ground-living warbler. It gets its name from its nest, which has a domed roof and is shaped like an old-fashioned oven—all made from grass and dead leaves and well hidden among vegetation.

Orange crown stripe

White throat

White belly with thick black streaks

Olive upperparts

In Florida, this bird sometimes follows armadillos to catch insects disturbed by their movements.

Northern waterthrush
Parkesia noveboracensis

Difficult to spot as it hides in thickets of dense swamps and bogs, the northern waterthrush has a habit of bobbing its head and tail.

Streaked belly

Dark stripe through the eye

Black-and-white warbler
Mniotilta varia

Behaving like a creeper or nuthatch, this bird hops along tree trunks and branches, probing the bark for insects.

Black throat in males, white in females

♂

Common yellowthroat
Geothlypis trichas

One of the most widespread of warblers in North America, the common yellowthroat is found mainly in wet, marshy habitats. It flits among the vegetation looking for small invertebrate prey, especially spiders.

Only males have a black face mask.

Yellow throat and belly in both sexes

♂

Yellow below tail

Flesh-colored legs

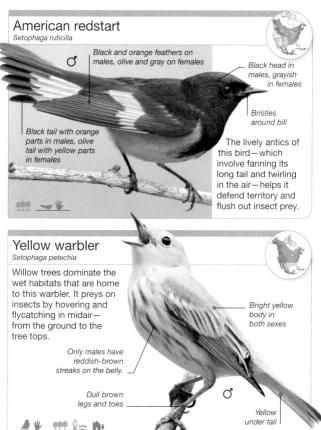

American redstart
Setophaga ruticilla

♂

Black and orange feathers on males, olive and gray on females

Black head in males, grayish in females

Bristles around bill

Black tail with orange parts in males, olive tail with yellow parts in females

The lively antics of this bird—which involve fanning its long tail and twirling in the air—helps it defend territory and flush out insect prey.

Yellow warbler
Setophaga petechia

Willow trees dominate the wet habitats that are home to this warbler. It preys on insects by hovering and flycatching in midair— from the ground to the tree tops.

Bright yellow body in both sexes

Only males have reddish-brown streaks on the belly.

Dull brown legs and toes

♂

Yellow under tail

Canada warbler
Cardellina canadensis

Yellow "spectacles" in males

The short northern summers give this warbler just a few months to breed in the cool coniferous forests before migrating the huge distance to overwinter in tropical South America.

Males have a thicker black "necklace" than females.

Both sexes have yellow underparts.

♂

White undertail feathers

Painted redstart
Myioborus pictus

By breeding in the warmer south, this warbler has a shorter distance to migrate than most other species—just as far as Mexico. Some birds even stay put all year round.

White patch below eye

White wing patch

Reddish-brown belly

This bird gets some of its water by drinking tree sap during springtime.

Cardinals and tanagers

The chunky bills of many cardinals show that they feed on seeds and fruit, while the thinner bills of tanagers are used mainly to forage for insects. This group includes some of the most brightly colored of all birds.

Scarlet tanager
Piranga olivacea

A striking summer visitor to North American forests, this bird lives and nests high in the trees, but it is often seen in open parkland when migrating. It spends winter in South American rain forests.

Dark brown eyes

Males are red and black, females are yellow

♂

Rose-breasted grosbeak
Pheucticus ludovicianus

This bird uses its thick bill to crush seeds and fruit, such as elderberry and mulberry, but eats more insects when nesting. It often visits gardens to take advantage of feeders.

Black and white feathers in males, brown in females

♂

Males have a red chest.

FOCUS ON...
COLOR
The red of a northern cardinal and blue of an indigo bunting show how birds produce color.

◀ Reds and yellows are caused by chemical pigments in the feathers—which may come from the bird's diet.

◀ Blues come from the way the structure of the feathers reflects or scatters light.

Painted bunting
Passerina ciris

Male painted buntings do not get their multicolored pattern until their second year—until then, they are green, like the mature females.

Violet-blue head

Red and green wings

Bright red underparts

♂

Dickcissel
Spiza americana

The dickcissel is a bird of the open grassland, where it nests in low vegetation. It gets its name from its *dick-dick-cissel-cissel* call, which can be a common summer sound heard on the prairies.

Black chin in males, absent in females

Reddish-brown shoulder in breeding males

♂

Tropical birds

Some birds that might be seen in North America are more at home in the tropics—but manage to survive in the warmer southern US states. Parts of the US—including Florida and the Hawaiian Islands—have a tropical climate all year round, so are home to many exotic species.

RARE BIRD
The Laysan finch—of the honeycreeper family—is found only on the remote Laysan Island in the Hawaiian chain.

Tropical waterbirds

Birds of the warmer Caribbean and Pacific coasts include exotic species, such as flamingos, tropicbirds, and spoonbills, that just reach mainland US shores. Florida's Everglades wetlands—which stretches into the tropics—is home to many.

American flamingo
Phoenicopterus ruber

Neck held out straight when flying

Pink color comes from animals it eats

The American flamingo lives in large colonies on Caribbean lagoons, where it uses its strange bill to strain tiny animals and build nests from mounds of mud. It is sometimes spotted in the Everglades.

Brown noddy
Anous stolidus

The brown noddy is found in the tropics around the world, but its only colony near the US is just south of Florida. It catches fish by dipping into the ocean surface.

Slender, dark bill

Gray head

Red-billed tropicbird
Phaethon aethereus

A graceful and acrobatic flier, the red-billed tropicbird spends much of its time over tropical seas, breeding on remote islands. It is sometimes spotted off the southeastern and southern California coasts.

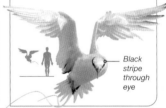

Black stripe through eye

Brown booby
Sula leucogaster

Boobies are tropical relatives of gannets—and, like them, plunge-dive into the ocean for fish. The brown booby lives in the Pacific and Caribbean, and might be seen in southern coastal states.

Long wings

Roseate spoonbill
Platalea ajaja

This wetland bird has its main range in tropical South America, but reaches the Gulf Coast. It sweeps the water with its bill to catch insects, shrimp, and fish.

Spoon-shaped bill

Red patch on pink wings

Bare skin on head

Tropical land birds

Tropical Central America is home to colorful quetzals and parrots that approach North America. Far into the Pacific, America's fiftieth state—Hawai'i—is home to birds found nowhere else, including an entire family of honeycreepers.

Eared quetzal
Euptilotis neoxenus

Quetzals are brightly colored birds of tropical forests, where they eat fruit and big insects. The eared quetzal lives in Mexico's hot dry pine forests—and just reaches into Arizona.

♂

Bluish-black head in males, browner in females

Thick-billed parrot   ENDANGERED
Rhynchopsitta pachyrhyncha

The loss of its Mexican pine forest habitat has endangered this bird, but it is being bred in captivity to increase numbers. It used to wander into Arizona and New Mexico, but has not been seen there since the 1990s.

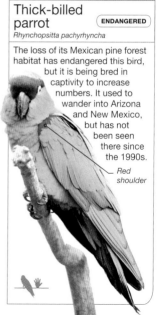

Red shoulder

'Akohekohe
Palmeria dolei   ENDANGERED

Like other members of the Hawaiian honeycreeper family, this bird feeds on nectar, and is threatened by loss of its forest habitat. It is only found on Maui Island, and it is critically endangered.

I'iwi
Drepanis coccinea

The I'iwi uses its long bill to probe the deepest flowers, but sometimes it pierces the base of a bloom to get at the nectar.

Curved bill

Scarlet feathers

'Akiapola'au   ENDANGERED
Hemignathus wilsoni

This honeycreeper's strange bill can do two jobs—the long, curved top part probes and rakes tree bark for insects and spiders, while the bottom part drills for sap.

Bright yellow head in males, olive in females

♂

Fascinating facts

NORTH AMERICAN RECORD BREAKERS

Biggest bird
At a size of 46–52 in (117–134 cm), the colossal California condor is larger than any other bird in North America. It soars the skies with a huge wingspan of 10 ft (3 m)—the largest on the continent.

Smallest bird
Measuring 3 in (7 cm) long, the calliope hummingbird is only about the size of a thumb. It has the smallest wingspan at 4 in (10 cm).

Tallest bird
Standing 5 ft (1.5 m) tall, the whooping crane is slightly shorter than the average adult person.

Lightest bird
The calliope hummingbird weighs only 0.09 oz (2.7 g), which is lighter than a grape!

Biggest beak
The American white pelican has the biggest beak, measuring up to 14 in (36.5 cm) in males.

Largest egg
The largest eggs are laid by the California condor and the trumpeter swan, at 4.5 in (11 cm) long.

Smallest egg
The egg of the calliope hummingbird is just 0.4 in (1 cm) long and even narrower!

Largest nest
The bald eagle takes three months to build its giant nest, spanning 6 ft (2 m) in diameter and weighing two tons.

Smallest nest
The calliope hummingbird makes a nest measuring 1.5 in (4 cm) to suit its small size.

Fastest runner
Topping 26 mph (42 kph), the greater roadrunner wins the race for the fastest bird on land.

The extinct passenger pigeon numbered about 3 billion in the early 19th century.

Fastest flyer
The fastest flying creature is the peregrine falcon, diving at jaw-dropping speeds of 242 mph (390 kph).

Longest nonstop migration
The bar-tailed godwit is known for the longest nonstop flight, migrating between Alaska and New Zealand, taking 11 days over 7,456 miles (12,000 km).

Most abundant bird
Birdwatchers are most likely to see an American robin, which has an estimated population of 300 million in North America.

AMAZING ABILITIES

Mighty migration
The Arctic tern flies from the Arctic to Antarctica—and back again—every year. This is a jaw-dropping distance of 55,000 miles (90,000 km)!

Eagle eyes
The bald eagle targets prey over long distances—up to 3 miles (4.8 km)—using its incredible eyesight, which is eight times stronger than human vision.

Marvel mimic
The northern mockingbird's noisy impressions range from car alarms and cell phones to squeaking doors and whistling trains.

Flapping flier
The tiny ruby-throated hummingbird has the fastest wings, flapping in flight about 53 times a second.

Hyper heart
Hummingbirds are known for their heartbeat, pulsing 1,200 times every minute while they hover.

Sound sleep
The common poorwill is the only bird known to hibernate.

Delightful display
The male frigatebird can inflate its throat to look like a big red balloon to impress females.

BIZARRE BEHAVIOR

• The **pileated woodpecker** uses its super-strong beak to peck up to 12,000 times a day.

• **Hummingbirds** are the only birds in the world capable of flying backward.

• **Ruby-throated hummingbirds** must eat half their body weight in sugar every day, so they feed every few hours.

• The **Canada jay** uses its sticky saliva to glue food to the branches of trees ready to eat later.

• **Killdeers** pretend to be injured if predators come close in order to draw them away from their eggs and chicks.

• **Grebes** eat their own feathers—this helps soften spiky fish bones.

• The male **American woodcock** can flap its wings to produce a tweeting sound that attracts females.

• **Western gulls** drop clams from dizzying heights, so they smash on the rocks and crack open.

• **Northern cardinals** mistake their own window reflections for other birds and try to fight themselves!

More about birds

NORTH AMERICAN BIRD RESERVES

Bosque Del Apache National Wildlife Refuge
Since 1939 this wildlife sanctuary in New Mexico has protected a variety of birds, such as sandhill cranes and golden eagles.

Cave Creek Canyon
About 370 types of bird inhabit Cave Creek Canyon in Arizona, including the elegant trogon and many species of hummingbirds.

Aransas National Wildlife Refuge
This Texas refuge presents a wintering home for endangered whooping cranes, and a range of shorebirds and wading birds.

Cape May Point Observatory
Set up in 1976, this New Jersey observatory stands on a peninsula offering an exceptional view of migrating songbirds, as well as falcons, hawks, ospreys, and warblers.

Magee Marsh
On the banks of Lake Erie in Ohio lies Magee Marsh, an important stop for thousands of songbirds migrating across the water every year.

Conservation efforts have increased the numbers of the rare California condor.

Hawk Mountain Sanctuary
Living up to its name, Hawk Mountain in Pennsylvania provides a safe haven for hawks, including broad-winged hawks and red-tailed hawks, as well as golden eagles and peregrine falcons.

Bonaventure Island
This Canadian island has a large nesting site for seabirds, including northern gannets and black-legged kittiwakes.

ENDANGERED BIRDS

According to the Red List of Threatened Species created by the International Union for Conservation of Nature (IUCN), 13 percent of birds around the world are threatened with extinction. Similarly, US Federal and State lists highlight birds that are endangered. These are the 10 most endangered North American birds according to these lists that apply to only the US:

1. Bermuda petrel
2. California condor
3. Snail kite
4. Whooping crane
5. Gunnison sage-grouse
6. Red-cockaded woodpecker
7. Golden-cheeked warbler
8. Kirtland's warbler
9. Roseate tern
10. Florida grasshopper sparrow

BIRD NAMES

• The **fulvous whistling-duck** is named after its distinctive whistling call.

• Meaning "beautiful king," **king eider** takes its regal name from the male's vivid orange and blue face.

• **Roadrunners** were given their name by drivers who spotted them running along roads at high speed.

• The **chimney swift** lives up to its name by building nests inside chimneys.

• A big appetite for oysters earned the **American oystercatcher** its name in the 18th century.

• **Bonaparte's gull** is named after 19th-century French naturalist Charles Lucien Bonaparte, a cousin of military leader and French emperor Napoleon Bonaparte.

• The piercing feeding call of young **eastern-screech owls** led to the bird's noisy name.

• The **red-eyed vireo** is a small songbird with eyes that change from brown to red in the first year of its life.

• The **American flamingo** with its vibrant pink feathers is named after the Spanish word flamenco, meaning "fire."

POPULAR CULTURE

• Hedwig was a **snowy owl** belonging to young wizard Harry Potter in J.K. Rowling's *Harry Potter* series.

• Road Runner is a cartoon **roadrunner** chased by enemy Wile E. Coyote in the *Looney Tunes* series.

• German composer Ludwig van Beethoven incorporated bird song in *Symphony No 6*, using clarinets to sound like the **common cuckoo**.

• Woody Woodpecker is a playful **pileated woodpecker** who brings fun and laughter to his own cartoon show.

• The popular video game series *Angry Birds* features many common birds, including a **cardinal**, a **loon**, and a **bluebird**.

Jimmy the raven was a famous film star who featured in about 1,000 movies in the 20th century.

MYTHS & LEGENDS

• The **common raven** features in the Inuit story of creation as the maker of the world and the bringer of light.

• In a tale told by the Tsimshian tribe of Alaska the mythical figure Raven punishes thieving **seagulls** by throwing them into a fire, burning their wing tips black.

• The Ojibwa tribe believe **common loons** inspire the sound of their flutes.

Glossary

Adaptation
A feature of a living thing that makes it suited to its surroundings and food, helping it survive.

Altricial Describing a bird chick that hatches from an egg blind, naked, and helpless.

Barring A pattern on a bird's feathers made up of lots of short stripes.

Broadleaf forest
A forest made up of trees with broad flat leaves, such as oak and maple, rather than the needlelike leaves of conifers.

Brood All the chicks produced by a female bird from one set of eggs.

Camouflage
The way an animal blends into its surroundings, which helps it hide.

Captive breeding
A way of saving rare species from extinction by keeping them in enclosures and encouraging them to breed there to increase their numbers.

Carcass The body of a dead animal.

Classify To put living things into groups according to their relationships. For instance, ducks and geese are classified together because they are closely related.

Clutch All the eggs produced by a female bird at a time.

Colony A group of animals living close together. Some bird colonies are made up of one species, such as flamingos. Others contain several different species, such as seabird colonies that have gulls and murres.

Coniferous forest
A forest mainly made up of conifer trees, such as pines or spruce, that usually have evergreen needlelike leaves.

Conservation
Protecting, preserving, or restoring the natural world, including its habitats and species.

Courtship A display, such as a song or a dance, that attracts a mate.

Crest A clump of long head feathers.

Deciduous A tree or forest that loses its leaves in winter or during the dry season.

Endangered
A species that is threatened with extinction.

Estuary Where a river flows into the sea.

Evergreen A tree or forest that keeps its leaves all year round.

Extinction When the last individual of a species dies.

Family A subgroup of an order, used in classifying living things.

Feeder Anything, such as a table or a hanging container, that is used to supply food for garden birds.

Fledging When a young bird grows flight feathers, which help it fly for the first time.

Flock A group of birds that are close together. A "mixed flock" is a group made up of more than one species.

Flycatching The way certain kinds of birds, such as tyrants, fly out to catch insects on the wing.

Granary An animal's store of nuts or seeds, such as when an acorn woodpecker stores nuts in tree trunk holes.

Habitat The type of place where a species lives within its range, such as grassland or forest.

Hibernation A long period of sleep that helps some kinds of animals survive the winter. The common poorwill is the only bird known to hibernate.

Incubation The way a bird sits on its eggs to keep them warm so they can develop and hatch.

Inshore Seas close to the land and visible from the shoreline.

Juvenile A young animal.

Kleptoparasite An animal, such as a frigatebird or jaeger, that steals its food from another.

Leaf litter A layer of dead leaves on the ground.

Mangrove A tree or forest that grows along the sea's salty coastline.

Migration An animal's regular journey between one place to another. North American bird migration usually involves birds flying between summer breeding places in the north to places for overwintering farther south.

Mimicry The way one kind of animal copies another. Some birds mimic the calls of others.

Mottled A pattern on a bird's feathers made up of lots of spots or dashes.

Molt Replacing one kind of plumage with another.

Nectar Sweet, sugar-rich liquid produced by flowers.

Nest box An artificial (human-made) box used by birds for nesting.

Nestling A chick that is in a nest.

Offshore Seas and oceans far from the coastline.

Order One of the main groups of birds and other living things, used in their classification.

Overwinter Spend the winter. Migratory birds overwinter in a place that is different from their summer breeding ranges.

Passerine A member of the largest group of birds, often called perching birds, including crows, warblers, and sparrows.

Pigment Colored substance.

Plumage A bird's coating of feathers.

Plunge-diving Diving down into water head first.

Precocial Describing a bird chick that hatches from an egg with fluffy feathers, opens its eyes, and can run soon afterward.

Predator An animal that kills and eats another.

Range The region where a species lives.

Raptor Bird of prey.

Sap Liquid running through a plant stem or tree trunk, which may contain a lot of sugar—like nectar.

Scavenger An animal that feeds on dead animals and other waste or discarded things.

Soaring A way of keeping in the air by letting outstretched wings catch the wind, without flapping them.

Species Kind of living or extinct thing. Members of the same species breed together to produce more of their own kind.

Talons Long, curved claws, used as weapons by many birds of prey.

Temperate A climate or part of the world that is between the very cold poles and hot tropics. Temperate places usually have warm summers and cold winters.

Tropical A climate or part of the world that is hot and wet throughout the year.

Tundra A kind of cold, open, treeless land found near Earth's poles, where the ground is frozen throughout the year.

Wetland A habitat that is flooded with water. Wooded wetlands are often called swamps.

Woodland Forest with plenty of open spaces between the trees.

Index

Acknowledgments

Dorling Kindersley would like to thank the following people for their help with making the book: Anne Lacy at the International Crane Foundation for information on the sandhill crane; Sreshtha Bhattacharya, Virien Chopra, Aman Kumar, Mrinal Pant, and Rupa Rao for editorial assistance; Anastasia Baliyan for design assistance; Nand Kishor Acharya for DTP design support; Saloni Singh and Priyanka Sharma Saddi for the jacket; Caroline Stamps for proofreading; and Helen Peters for the index.

The publisher would like to thank the following for their kind permission to reproduce their photographs:

(Key: a-above; b-below/bottom; c-center; f-far; l-left; r-right; t-top)

123RF.com: agamiphoto 138cla, gonepaddling 46bl, G2cl, 52bl, jgroup / James Steidl 16bc, avgogrecon 29cla; **Alamy Stock Photo:** AGAMI Photo Agency / Brian E. Small 71br, All Canada Photos / Glenn Bartley 29br, 39fr, 67r, All Canada Photos / Tim Zurowski 76bl, All Canada Photos / Wayne Lynch 38clb (common poorwill), Don Johnston_BI 32b, Steven Kovacs / Biosphoto 102cb, Blue Planet Archive SLE-X 138bc, Rick & Nora Bowers 129cla, Janice and Nolan Braud 17t, Gay Bumgarner 8-9, Monkey Business 142cr, Cloudybright / Carmen K. Sisson 17crb, Phil Degginger 4bc, Danita Delimont 169bc, Design Pics Inc / Milo Burcham 27tr, infocusphotos.com / Malie Rich-Griffith 43tl, 43tc, 43tr, Jack Jeffrey / BIA / Minden Pictures 147br, James Mundy, Nature's Ark Photography 106cla, William Leaman 11tc, 98-99, Rodrigo Friscione / Cultura Creative Ltd 75bc, blickwinkel / M. Woike 87br, Minden Pictures / BIA / Alan Murphy 38clb, Minden Pictures / BIA / Glenn Bartley 100tr, Minden Pictures / BIA / Tim Zurowski 33br, Alan Murphy / BIA / Minden Pictures 171br / Brian E Small 31cla, Nature Picture Library / Claudio Contreras 144cl, Nature Picture Library / Luke Massey 155ca, Steve Oehlenschlager 29cra, Photo Resource Hawaii 143bc, Rolf Nussbaumer Photography 119cb, Jack Jeffrey / BIA / Minden Pictures 147cra, Lee Rentz 146clb, Roberta Olenick / All Canada Photos 92bl, Rolf Nussbaumer Photography 113bl, SBS Eclectic Images 16cr, Janet Griffin-Scott 89tr, Smitty Smitty 122-123c, Marco Valentini 57b, Tom Walker 40-41, Wildscotphotos 128cb; **Dorling Kindersley:** Robert Royse 139cb; **Dreamstime.com:**

135bl, 100bl, Andreanita 16cb (kittiwake), Andreistanescu 6cra, 9tr, Anthonyferrana6901 24bl, Rinua Baak 73cla, Rinus Baak 50b, 52bc, 72cb, Rejean Bedard 11tr, Kristian Bell 51cla, Steven Blandin 71t, Lukas Blazek 27br, 36b, Bmatheson 111cl, 11clb, Karel Bock 5cra, 85br, 119ca, Paul Brennan 53ca, Charles Brutlag 106clb, Steve Byland 31br, 77br, 33ca, 85cra, 127cla, 15cr, 109br, 79b, Lynn Bystrom 92ca, Dee Carpenter 48clb, 11crb, Howard Cheek 115br, Jason Cheever 116bl, Harry Collins 45cb, 95bc, 145br, 15bl, 78, 79cra, 101c, Dorothy Merrimon Crawford 11cra, Sandi Cullifer 22clb, Jim Cumming 47cra, 133cra, 66c, Eric Dale 63bl, 7br, Daviesjk 23b, Gerald Deboer 37br, 43br, 51br, 145cla, Dml231 13br, Donyanedomam 24cra, 26b, 103br, Leola Durant 56br, Kent Ellington 16cb (crane), Michael Elliott 11cr, John Fader 18bc, Sue Feldberg 129cb, Joe Ferrer 49b, K Quinn Ferris 111cr, Frank Fichtmueller 125ca, Randy Fletcher 114b, 126c, 7bc, 11cla, Sophia Granichmino 128clb, Grayfoxx1942 7bl, 88bl, Tero Hakala 83t, Hakoar 46-47bc, 73crb, 134fbr, Bipul Haldar 72cl, Linda Harms 4bl, Yuval Helfman 43clb, Helgidinson 133cl, 1, 134cra, Hellmann1 28br, Chris Hill 131cra, Rachel Hopper 1clb, 7cl, Mark Hryciw 24cla, 112cr, 10b, Ivkuzmin 63br, 112bl, 124cb, Jerryway 11br, Jhaviv 146crb, Jocrebbin 48bl, Trevor Jones 15br, Bill Kennedy 70br, Brian Kushner 51cra, 84cl, 103bl, 116br, Jean Landry 108bl, Brian Lasenby 23cla, 53cla, 65cb, 84cb, 130ca, 133br, 135cra, 76c, 107, Caleb Lawson 18br, Leerobin 88br, 14cr, Stephen Linton 61crb, Lorierda 49tl, Paula Masterson 77l, Sander Meesters 81cla, Steven Melanson 6br, Melodyanne 18-19c, Christophe Merceron 120c, Mikelane45 23cra, 53b, 82bl, 1411l, 11cl, Michael Mill 107tl, Mirkorosenau 22br, Daniel Montesi 14br, Natakuzmina 63cra, 106cr, 97cla, Nozyer 47br, Npage 13tr, (null) (null) 15cl, Passiondenature 28bl, Martin Pelanek 82crb, 137cla, 70bl, Peterll 107br, Jay Pierstorff 42br, 103tc, Glenn Price 30bl, Steven Prorak 22cl, Ondřej Prosický 93br, Paul Reeves 27bl, 30br, 37t, 39bl, 111bl, 117ca, 117bc, 119br, 124cca, 125bc, 137crb, 121cra, 9fbr, 15cra, 108br, 97cr, Dan Rieck 15c, Patrick Rolands 89cra, Saurabh13 140bl, Saxonsfoto 63cla, 79cla, Smitty4114 48c, Paul Sparks 21cb, 109tr, David Spates 121cla, 129cra, 131cb, Vadim Startsev 119bl, Harold Stiver 60br, 140br, 7c, 10cra, 16cb (albatross), Nancy Strohm 38br, 147clb, Stubblefieldphoto 14bl, Svetlana Foote 14bc, Gerald D. Tang 113br, 82bl, Tarpan 59cra, 59br, Tinamou 69b, Txgrapricdesign 16cla, Tupungato 61cra, Gale Verhague 130ca, 141bl, 16c, Vfab99 141tr, Rebecca Warren 97bl, William Wise 5bl, 137bl, Paul Wolf 11bl, 76br, Feng Yu

6bl, 56ca, Razvan Zinica 128bl; **Getty Images:** Sharif Uddin / 500px 145cra, CR Courson / Moment Open 89cl, Troy Harrison / Moment 90-91, Tze-hsin Woo / Moment 86b, Moment / mallardg500 12b, Moment / Photography by Alexandra Rudge 35cb, Moment / Scott Suriano 25b, Moment / Vicki Jauron, Babylon and Beyond Photography 54-55c, www.harshadventure.com / Moment 93cra, Paul Souders 59cla; **Getty Images / iStock:** ablokhin 64c, AGAMI stock 132cb, 136c, Rejean Bedard 130cb, BirdImages 44, 121crb, Jeremy Carpenter 19cra, Gerald Corsi 68, drferry 72fcb, dypics 69cla, 15bc, E+ / Kelvinca13cl, pchoui / E+ 89br, Jeff Edwards / Getty Images Plus 85cla, GarysFRP 20, kojihirano / Getty Images Plus 110bc, photographybyJHWilliams / Getty Images Plus 113tr, moose henderson 87tc, photosbyash 77cra, Linda Koski / Getty Images Plus 84crb, MattCuda 42tl, OldFulica 83tc, pchoui / E+ 134cl, Christina Radcliffe / Getty Images Plus 104, RT-Images 127fbr, Sundry Photography 14c, Supercaliphotolistic 62cb, Flavio Vallenari 140t, WalterSpina 13bc, wwing 5br; **naturepl.com:** Alan Murphy / BIA 94, Alan Murphy 96, 34, Jack Dykinga 80, Scott Leslie 16br. **Shutterstock.com:** Agami Photo Agency 59br, 87bl, Mircea Costina 115cla, TPCImagery - Mike Jackson 85bc, Nick Pecker 58b

Cover images:
Front: **123RF.com:** pkzoregon; **Dorling Kindersley:** Chris Gomersall Photography, Tom Grey, Liberty's Owl, Raptor and Reptile Centre, Hampshire, UK, Alan Murphy, E. J. Peiker, Roger Tidman; **Dreamstime.com:** John Anderson, Bmatheson, Steve Byland, Howard Cheek, Jim Cumming, Donyanedomam, Ed8563, Loren Fife, Randy Fletcher, Hakoar, Isselee, Ivkuzmin, Bill Kennedy, Jean Landry, Brian Lasenby, Liacmiao, Daniel Logan, Christophe Merceron, Mikelane45, Natakuzmina, Jay Pierstorff, Alexander Potapov, Ondej Prosick, Paul Reeves, Saurabh13, Paul Sparks, David Spates, Suebmtl, Gerald D. Tang, Thomas Torget, Rebecca Warren; **Fotolia:** Stefan Zeitz / Lux; **Getty Images / iStock:** AGAMI stock, photography by JHWilliams

Front & Spine: **naturepl.com:** Jan Wegener

All other images © Dorling Kindersley
For further information see:
www.dkimages.com